From MANGER to MESSIAH

AN ADVENT FAMILY BIBLE STUDY

Taylor Turner

CLAY BRIDGES
PRESS

From Manger to Messiah: An Advent Family Bible Study

Copyright © 2025 by Taylor Turner

Published by Clay Bridges Press in Houston, TX

www.ClayBridgesPress.com

All rights reserved. No part of this publication may be reproduced, stored in a retrieval system, or transmitted in any form by any means, electronic, mechanical, photocopy, recording, or otherwise, without the prior permission of the publisher, except as provided for by USA copyright law.

Unless otherwise indicated, scripture quotations are taken from the CEV® Bible (Contemporary English Version) Copyright © 1991, 1992, 1995 by American Bible Society, Used by Permission.

Scripture quotations marked (GNT) are from the Good News Translation in Today's English Version- Second Edition Copyright © 1992 by American Bible Society. Used by Permission.

Scripture quotations marked (KJV) are taken from the King James Version (KJV): King James Version, public domain.

Scripture quotations marked (NIV) are taken from the Holy Bible, New International Version®, NIV®. Copyright ©1973, 1978, 1984, 2011 by Biblica, Inc.™ Used by permission of Zondervan. All rights reserved worldwide. www.zondervan.com The "NIV" and "New International Version" are trademarks registered in the United States Patent and Trademark Office by Biblica, Inc.™

ISBN: 978-1-68488-145-1
eISBN: 978-1-68488-146-8

Special Sales: Most Clay Bridges titles are available in special quantity discounts. Custom imprinting or excerpting can also be done to fit special needs. Contact Clay Bridges at Info@ClayBridgesPress.com

To my precious gifts, Saint and Legend: This family Bible study is written with you in mind. You are living reminders of God's grace. I dedicate this journey through His Word to you.

Love y'all!

Special Thanks

Thank You, Jesus. You saw me at my worst, loved me through it, and made me new. Without You, this book wouldn't exist, and I surely wouldn't be here to write it. Thank You for Your grace that covers my past and Your love that carries me forward.

To my husband Travis, my rock and real-life teammate: Thank you for standing beside me in the chaos and the calm. Whether you're on the field coaching or helping me wrangle toddlers, you're my biggest blessing.

To my three wonderful kids: You are the reason this study exists. To my little wild boy, my curious five-year-old girl, and my beautiful stepdaughter: You have taught me more about God's love than any textbook ever could. Thank you for being my inspiration, my why; I love y'all with all my heart.

To my sister Daniella and my mom Velma: Thank you for cheering me on, praying over this book, and helping me believe this could happen. Your encouragement kept me moving on days when doubt was loud.

And to every parent reading this book: Thank you for letting me be part of your family's walk with Jesus. What a gift.

Contents

A Note from the Author ix

Tips for Advent Bible Study xi

Day 1: Luke 1 – An Angel Brings Good News 1

Day 2: Luke 2 – The Birth of Jesus..9

Day 3: Luke 3 – John Prepares the Way......................................18

Day 4: Luke 4 – Jesus Says No to Temptation.............................28

Day 5: Luke 5 – Jesus Chooses His Helpers................................38

Day 6: Luke 6 – Jesus Teaches about Love..................................47

Day 7: Luke 7 – Jesus Helps and Heals 57

Day 8: Luke 8 – Jesus's Power over Nature................................66

Day 9: Luke 9 – Jesus Feeds Thousands......................................78

Day 10: Luke 10 – The Good Neighbor......................................89

Day 11: Luke 11 – Teach Us to Pray...98

Day 12: Luke 12 – Don't Worry..110

Day 13: Luke 13 – God's Growing Kingdom 119

Day 14: Luke 14 – A Special Invitation..127

Day 15: Luke 15 – The Lost and Found 134

Day 16: Luke 16 – Being Faithful 141

Day 17: Luke 17 – The Grateful One...148

Day 18: Luke 18 – Come to Jesus 155

Day 19: Luke 19 – Jesus Loves Everyone 163

Day 20: Luke 20 – Listening to Jesus..172

Day 21: Luke 21 – Jesus Is Coming Again...180

Day 22: Luke 22 – The Last Supper 188

Day 23: Luke 23 – Jesus Dies for Us...198

Day 24: Luke 24 – Jesus Is Alive!..206

Chapter Activities and Recipes...217

Bible Trivia: Family Feud Style Rules..233

Endnotes..245

A Note from the Author

Hey there! I am Taylor Turner. I'm a wife, mom of three, and science teacher who loves Jesus, coffee, and cheering at ball games. I'm married to a wonderful teacher and sports coach. Our family includes a busy toddler boy; an energetic, sassy five-year-old girl; and a beautiful twenty-year-old stepdaughter. Our home is loud, lively, and full of love (and snacks).

At thirty-three, I have lived through some ups and downs. My past isn't perfect, but Jesus met me right where I was and changed everything. Now, I do my best every day to help my family know and love Him too.

I created this Bible study to bring faith and fun together. Whether you're cuddling up with your kids, digging into Scripture, or having conversations around the dining table, I hope this book helps you grow together in God's love. Parenting isn't always easy, but it's beautiful when Jesus is in the middle of it.

Tips for Advent Bible Study

- Set aside time each night of December or any night as a family to read God's Word and learn about the life of Jesus. This could be your time to talk about the true meaning of Christmas and of life—a time of learning to live and love like Jesus.

- Pray together as a family to start each reading. Each day's reading includes an opening and closing prayer, which you may choose to use for starters. But hopefully, by the end of the book, you and your family will have confidence to pray on your own.

- Pray that this study would help you and your family know Jesus more deeply and that the Word would transform your hearts and help you grow closer as a family and closer to God.

- Put all phones and technology aside during your daily study and let your focus be on His Word.

- Have fun and really get involved in the discussions. Questions should be answered by both adults and kids. Parents/Adults, go first and give examples; then make sure kids get involved in discussions.

- It helps when parents/adults share first. The purpose of *Advent Family Bible Study* is all about knowing the story of Jesus, but I would love for you and your families to grow closer together in the process.

- Feel free to vary how you approach each day's Scripture reading. You may assign one person to read the whole chapter or take turns reading through the passage. That is totally up to you.

- Give everyone an opportunity to share an answer for each question. You can pick a couple of questions to discuss or discuss all the questions.

- You can use one copy of the study for the whole family, or each person can have their own copy so they can write down their answers before the discussion and then share during discussion time. The latter may make the discussion move along more quickly.

- Don't put too much stress on doing the study every night; if you miss one, that is totally fine. Although I wrote this as an Advent Bible Study for the season leading up to Christmas, you can use this any time of the year and split it up if you would like. Jesus just wants to be closer to you and your family, and this is a great place to start, whether you choose to do the study every day for twenty-four days straight or once or twice a week.

- Some questions are repeated throughout the Bible study because I wanted to stress the major themes in Luke's Gospel. As you work through the study, you may choose to answer the questions the same way you did **initially,** or you can answer them differently and give new examples.

- The final section of the book includes fun activities and snack ideas that go with the content of each chapter. The reading and activities and snacks do not have to be done on the same day; feel free to do the related activities on a different day as a time of review and reflection as a way of breaking the study and activities into manageable segments.

Day 1

Luke 1 – An Angel Brings Good News

Memory Verse of the Week: *"Nothing is impossible for God"* (Luke 1:37)!

Remember that all things are possible when God is in the mix. Say the memory verse together as a family. Then ask everyone to write the verse down a few times and put it on a sticky note in a visible location (e.g., on the bathroom mirror or as the background on their cell phones).

Make sure to quiz each other throughout the week and encourage one another. For younger kids this can be something you practice before bedtime. Talk about why this verse is important and when it can be helpful. It is good to have a memory verse in your pocket to remind yourself of God's Word and goodness. You got this!

> **Opening Prayer:** *Dear God, thank You for always keeping Your promises, just like You did for Zechariah and Mary. As we read chapter 1 of Luke's Gospel together, help us remember that You are faithful, even when we don't understand Your plan. Open our hearts to trust You more as a family. Help us talk about what we learn and grow closer to You and to each other. In Jesus's name, we pray. Amen.*

Luke 1:1-25 (GNT)

¹ Dear Theophilus: Many people have done their best to write a report of the things that have taken place among us. ² They wrote what we have been told by those who saw these things from the beginning and who proclaimed the message. ³ And so, Your Excellency, because I have carefully studied all these matters from their beginning, I thought it would be good to write an orderly account for you. ⁴ I do this so that you will know the full truth about everything which you have been taught. ⁵ During the time when Herod was king of Judea, there was a priest named Zechariah, who belonged to the priestly order of Abijah. His wife's name was Elizabeth; she also belonged to a priestly family. ⁶ They both lived good lives in God's sight and obeyed fully all the Lord's laws and commands. ⁷ They had no children because Elizabeth could not have any, and she and Zechariah were both very old. ⁸ One day Zechariah was doing his work as a priest in the Temple, taking his turn in the daily service. ⁹ According to the custom followed by the priests, he was chosen by lot to burn incense on the altar. So he went into the Temple of the Lord, ¹⁰ while the crowd of people outside prayed during the hour when the incense was burned. ¹¹ An angel of the Lord appeared to him, standing at the right side of the altar where the incense was burned. ¹² When Zechariah saw him, he was alarmed and felt afraid. ¹³ But the angel said to him, "Don't be afraid, Zechariah! God has heard your prayer, and your wife Elizabeth will bear you a son. You are to name him John. ¹⁴ How glad and happy you will be, and how happy many others

Luke 1 – An Angel Brings Good News

will be when he is born! ¹⁵ John will be great in the Lord's sight. He must not drink any wine or strong drink. From his very birth he will be filled with the Holy Spirit, ¹⁶ and he will bring back many of the people of Israel to the Lord their God. ¹⁷ He will go ahead of the Lord, strong and mighty like the prophet Elijah. He will bring fathers and children together again; he will turn disobedient people back to the way of thinking of the righteous; he will get the Lord's people ready for him." ¹⁸ Zechariah said to the angel, "How shall I know if this is so? I am an old man, and my wife is old also." ¹⁹ "I am Gabriel," the angel answered. "I stand in the presence of God, who sent me to speak to you and tell you this good news. ²⁰ But you have not believed my message, which will come true at the right time. Because you have not believed, you will be unable to speak; you will remain silent until the day my promise to you comes true." ²¹ In the meantime the people were waiting for Zechariah and wondering why he was spending such a long time in the Temple. ²² When he came out, he could not speak to them, and so they knew that he had seen a vision in the Temple. Unable to say a word, he made signs to them with his hands. ²³ When his period of service in the Temple was over, Zechariah went back home. ²⁴ Some time later his wife Elizabeth became pregnant and did not leave the house for five months. ²⁵ "Now at last the Lord has helped me," she said. "He has taken away my public disgrace!"

Fill in the blanks as a family before you continue:

- An angel named _____ appeared to Zechariah while he was serving as a priest in the temple, telling him that his wife, Elizabeth, would bear a son named _____, even though they were both very old.

  Answer: (Gabriel, John)

- Because Zechariah doubted the angel's message, he was unable to _____ until the day the child was _____.

  Answer: (speak, born)

Luke 1:26-41 (GNT)

26 In the sixth month of Elizabeth's pregnancy God sent the angel Gabriel to a town in Galilee named Nazareth. 27 He had a message for a young woman promised in marriage to a man named Joseph, who was a descendant of King David. Her name was Mary. 28 The angel came to her and said, "Peace be with you! The Lord is with you and has greatly blessed you!" 29 Mary was deeply troubled by the angel's message, and she wondered what his words meant. 30 The angel said to her, "Don't be afraid, Mary; God has been gracious to you. 31 You will become pregnant and give birth to a son, and you will name him Jesus. 32 He will be great and will be called the Son of the Most High God. The Lord God will make him a king, as his ancestor David was, 33 and he will be the king of the descendants of Jacob forever; his kingdom will never end!" 34 Mary said to the angel, "I am a virgin. How, then, can this be?" 35 The angel answered, "The Holy

Spirit will come on you, and God's power will rest upon you. For this reason the holy child will be called the Son of God. ³⁶ Remember your relative Elizabeth. It is said that she cannot have children, but she herself is now six months pregnant, even though she is very old. ³⁷ For there is nothing that God cannot do." ³⁸ "I am the Lord's servant," said Mary; "may it happen to me as you have said." And the angel left her. ³⁹ Soon afterward Mary got ready and hurried off to a town in the hill country of Judea. ⁴⁰ She went into Zechariah's house and greeted Elizabeth. ⁴¹ When Elizabeth heard Mary's greeting, the baby moved within her. Elizabeth was filled with the Holy Spirit.

Fill in the blanks before you continue as a family.

- The angel told Mary that she will give birth to a son, whom she was to name _____ , and that he would be called the Son of the _____ .

    Answer: (Jesus, God)

- When Mary visited Elizabeth, the baby in Elizabeth _____ within her.

    Answer: (moved)

Family and Kid-Friendly Questions for Discussion

1. What would you do if an angel appeared to you like Gabriel did to Zechariah and Mary? How would you react if the angel told you something that seemed impossible?

   Parent/Adult Tip: It's okay if your child imagines being scared, surprised, or even confused; Zechariah and Mary were too. Use this question to talk about how God often speaks in ways that challenge our expectations. Emphasize that it's normal to have questions when God asks us to trust Him, but He wants us to respond with open hearts like Mary did. Help kids see that God still speaks today, through His Word, people, and quiet moments in our hearts.

   Ask: How would you feel if God asked you to do something that seemed too big or too hard? Do you think it's okay to ask questions like Mary did? Why do you think Zechariah lost his voice when he didn't believe? Can you think of a time when you had to trust someone even though you didn't understand everything? How can we practice trusting God even when things don't make sense?

2. Zechariah and Elizabeth were too old to have a baby, but God made it possible. What does that tell us about God?

   Parent/Adult Tip: Use this moment to help your children understand that God is powerful and trustworthy, even when His timing or plan doesn't make sense to us. Encourage your kids to look for everyday "miracles" such as answered prayers, protection, healing, or even the blessing of family and friends. For older kids or teens, gently guide them to reflect on things they've overcome or blessings they've seen after times of waiting. This builds their faith.

Ask: What does it mean that nothing is impossible for God? Have you ever prayed for something and God answered in a way that surprised you? Why do you think God waited so long to give Zechariah and Elizabeth a baby? How can we keep trusting God even when we don't see His answers right away? What is something you're praying for now?

3. What does Mary's response to the angel teach us about trusting God? How can we have courage like Mary did when the angels appeared?

   Parent/Adult Tip: Mary was likely a teenager, just like some of your kids, when she was given a huge, life-changing message. She could've been overwhelmed, scared, or full of questions, but she chose faith over fear. Talk to your children about times when they've felt nervous, scared, or unsure and how choosing trust (as Mary did) helped or could help them move forward. This helps kids of all ages see that bravery doesn't mean you're not scared; it means you trust God more than your fear.

   Ask: How do you think Mary felt when the angel showed up? How would you feel? What makes someone brave? Have you ever had to do something hard or scary, but you did it anyway? Why do you think Mary said yes to God even when she didn't understand everything? What are some things we can do when we feel scared or nervous (e.g., praying, talking to someone, or remembering God's promises)?

4. What can Zechariah's story teach us about having faith in God while still having doubts?

   Parent/Adult Tip: Zechariah was a good man who loved God, but even he had doubts when the angel told him something that seemed impossible. Sometimes, we try to figure everything out on our own, and that can make it hard to trust God's ways. Remind your kids that God doesn't always work the way we expect. His ways are higher, and sometimes we just need to believe even when we don't see how things will work out. Use this time to talk about how growing in faith comes from learning about who God is, reading His Word, and spending time talking to Him.

   Ask: Why do you think Zechariah had a hard time believing the angel? Have you ever had trouble trusting that God would help you with something? What can we do when we're having a hard time believing? Why do you think God kept His promise to Zechariah even though he doubted?

5. When Mary visited Elizabeth, the baby inside Elizabeth jumped for joy. How do you think families can bless and encourage each other today?

   Parent/Adult Tip: Mary and Elizabeth's visit wasn't just a casual moment; it was full of joy and shared excitement over what God was doing in their lives. In the same way, families today can encourage one another by showing up, listening, praying together, and speaking kind words. Explain to your kids that our presence and words can bring joy to someone else just like Mary's presence brought joy to Elizabeth. Helping kids see their role in blessing others, even as children or teens, empowers them to live out their faith every day.

Ask: Why do you think Elizabeth was so excited when Mary visited her? What are some ways we can bring joy to someone in our family this week? When has someone in our family helped you feel better or reminded you of God's love? What kind words could we say to encourage each other today?

> **Closing Prayer:** *Lord, thank You for showing us that nothing is impossible with You. Just like You used ordinary people to do extraordinary things in the Bible, we know You can work in our lives too. Help our family trust Your timing and believe that You have good plans for each of us. Let us encourage one another and grow in faith together. In Your name, we pray. Amen.*

Day 2

Luke 2 – The Birth of Jesus

Challenge: Can anyone say the memory verse without looking it up? Repeat the memory verse as a family.

Memory Verse of the Week: *"Nothing is impossible for God"* (Luke 1:37)!

> **Opening Prayer:** *Heavenly Father, thank You for the gift of Jesus. As we read about His birth, help us feel the joy and peace He brings. Let our home be filled with the same wonder the shepherds felt. In Jesus's name, we pray. Amen.*

Luke 2:1-21

[1] About that time Emperor Augustus gave orders for the names of all the people to be listed in record books. [2] These first records were made when Quirinius was governor of Syria. [3] Everyone had to go to their own hometown to be listed. [4] So Joseph had to leave Nazareth in Galilee and go to Bethlehem in Judea. Long ago Bethlehem had been King David's hometown, and Joseph went there because he was from David's family. [5] Mary was engaged to Joseph and traveled with him to Bethlehem. She was soon going to have a baby, [6] and while they were there, [7] she gave birth to her firstborn son. She dressed him in baby clothes and laid him on a bed of hay, because there was no room for them in the inn. [8] That night in the fields near Bethlehem some shepherds were guarding their sheep. [9] All at once an angel came down to them from the Lord, and the brightness of the Lord's glory flashed around them. The shepherds were frightened. [10] But the angel said, "Don't be afraid! I have good news for you, which will make everyone happy. [11] This very day in King David's hometown a Savior was born for you. He is Christ the Lord. [12] You will know who he is, because you will find him dressed in baby clothes and lying on a bed of hay." [13]

Luke 2 – The Birth of Jesus

Suddenly many other angels came down from heaven and joined in praising God. They said: ¹⁴ "Praise God in heaven! Peace on earth to everyone who pleases God." ¹⁵ After the angels had left and gone back to heaven, the shepherds said to each other, "Let's go to Bethlehem and see what the Lord has told us about." ¹⁶ They hurried off and found Mary and Joseph, and they saw the baby lying on a bed of hay. ¹⁷ When the shepherds saw Jesus, they told his parents what the angel had said about him. ¹⁸ Everyone listened and was surprised. ¹⁹ But Mary kept thinking about all this and wondering what it meant. ²⁰ As the shepherds returned to their sheep, they were praising God and saying wonderful things about him. Everything they had seen and heard was just as the angel had said. ²¹ Eight days later Jesus' parents did for him what the Law of Moses commands. And they named him Jesus, just as the angel had told Mary when he promised she would have a baby.

Fill in the blanks as a family before you continue:

- While Mary and Joseph were in _____ , the time came for Mary to give birth, and she laid her firstborn son in a bed of _____ .

   Answer: (Bethlehem, hay)

- An angel appeared to shepherds in the fields, telling them that a _____ had been born in Bethlehem, who is Christ the _____ .

   Answer: (Savior, Lord)

Luke 2:22-40

²² The time came for Mary and Joseph to do what the Law of Moses says a mother is supposed to do after her baby is born. They took Jesus to the temple in Jerusalem and presented him to the Lord, ²³ just as the Law of the Lord says, "Each first-born baby boy belongs to the Lord." ²⁴ The Law of the Lord also says parents have to offer a sacrifice, giving at least a pair of doves or two young pigeons. So that is what Mary and Joseph did. ²⁵ At this time a man named Simeon was living in Jerusalem. Simeon was a good man. He loved God and was waiting for him to save the people of Israel. God's Spirit came to him ²⁶ and told him that he would not die until he had seen Christ the Lord. ²⁷ When Mary and Joseph brought Jesus to the temple to do what the Law of Moses says should be done, ²⁸ Simeon took the baby Jesus in his arms and praised God, ²⁹ "Lord, I am your servant, and now I can die in peace, because you have kept your promise to me. ³⁰ With my own eyes I have seen what you have done to save your people, ³¹ and foreign nations will also see this. ³² Your mighty power is a light for all nations, and it will bring honor to your people Israel." ³³ Jesus' parents were surprised at what Simeon had said. ³⁴ Then he blessed them and told Mary, "This child of yours will cause many people in Israel to fall and others to stand. The child will be like a warning sign. Many people will reject him, ³⁵ and you, Mary, will suffer as though you had been stabbed by a dagger. But all this will show what people are really thinking."

³⁶ The prophet Anna was also there in the temple. She was the daughter of Phanuel from the tribe of Asher, and she

was very old. In her youth she had been married for seven years, ³⁷ but her husband died, and now she was 84 years old. Night and day she served God in the temple by praying and often going without eating. ³⁸ At that time Anna came in and praised God. She spoke about the child Jesus to everyone who hoped for Jerusalem to be set free. ³⁹ After Joseph and Mary had done everything that the Law of the Lord commands, they returned home to Nazareth in Galilee. ⁴⁰ The child Jesus grew. He became strong and wise, and God blessed him.

Fill in the blanks a family before you continue:

- When the time came, Mary and Joseph took Jesus to the _____ to present him to the Lord, as required by the law of _____ .

  Answer: (temple, Moses)

- A good man named _____ was in the temple. The Holy Spirit had revealed to him that he would not die until he had seen Christ the _____ .

  Answer: (Simeon, Lord)

Luke 2:41-52

⁴¹ Every year Jesus' parents went to Jerusalem for Passover. ⁴² And when Jesus was twelve years old, they all went there as usual for the celebration. ⁴³ After Passover his parents left, but they did not know that Jesus had stayed on in the city. ⁴⁴ They thought he was traveling with some other people,

and they went a whole day before they started looking for him. ⁴⁵ When they could not find him with their relatives and friends, they went back to Jerusalem and started looking for him there. ⁴⁶ Three days later they found Jesus sitting in the temple, listening to the teachers and asking them questions. ⁴⁷ Everyone who heard him was surprised at how much he knew and at the answers he gave. ⁴⁸ When his parents found him, they were amazed. His mother said, "Son, why have you done this to us? Your father and I have been very worried, and we have been searching for you!" ⁴⁹ Jesus answered, "Why did you have to look for me? Didn't you know that I would be in my Father's house?" ⁵⁰ But they did not understand what he meant. ⁵¹ Jesus went back to Nazareth with his parents and obeyed them. His mother kept on thinking about all that had happened. ⁵² Jesus became wise, and he grew strong. God was pleased with him and so were the people.

Fill in the blanks as a family before you continue:

- Jesus's parents found him after _____ days of searching, and Mary asked him, "Why have you _____ this to us?"

Answer: (Three days, done)

- Jesus replied, "Didn't you know that I would be in my _____ ," but they did not understand what he meant.

Answer: (father's house)

Luke 2 – The Birth of Jesus

Family and Kid-Friendly Questions for Discussion

1. Why do you think Jesus was born in such a simple place as a stable or bed of hay?

   Parent/Adult Tip: Jesus, the King of kings, was not born in a palace or surrounded by riches. He came into the world in the humblest way possible, showing us that God values humility, love, and being close to everyone, not just the rich or important. Remind your kids that Jesus's birth in a simple stable teaches us that God meets us where we are, no matter our background and that greatness doesn't come from where you're born or what you have, but from how you live and love. Encourage your children and teens to think about what humility looks like in their own lives and how Jesus's birth story helps them see others with compassion.

   Ask: How does it make you feel knowing Jesus didn't come to earth in a fancy place but in a stable? Where would you typically picture Jesus being born if you were told he was the king? Does this story help you see people who have less in a different way? If Jesus visited our home today, how could we make Him feel welcome, not with stuff but with our hearts and actions?

2. How do you think Mary and Joseph felt when they couldn't find a place to stay?

   Parent/Adult Tip: Help your kids imagine how stressful, scary, and uncomfortable it must have been for Mary and Joseph. They were far from home; Mary was about to give birth, and everywhere they went, they were told that there was "no room."

And yet, God still had a plan, even if it didn't look like it was going to work out. Use this opportunity to remind your children that God is with us even in life's messy or disappointing moments. When things don't go our way, we can still trust Him to work it all out for good. This is a great time to connect and share your own experiences with facing unexpected situations and how God helped you through them.

Ask: What do you think Mary and Joseph were thinking or feeling when everyone said there was no room? Have you ever felt left out or like something wasn't fair? What did you do? Why do you think God allowed Jesus to be born in such a difficult situation? What can you do when life feels hard or confusing as it must have for Mary and Joseph? Parent/Adults, how would you feel if this happened to you?

3. What would you have done to help Mary and Joseph if you had been there?

    Parent/Adult Tip: Use this question to talk about kindness, compassion, and looking out for others, especially when they're in need. This is a great chance to plant seeds of empathy in your child's heart and encourage them to think of ways to be helpful today. (*Empathy* is the ability to understand and share the feelings of another person.)

    Ask: If you saw a tired couple with no place to stay, what would you do to help them? Can you think of someone today who might need help or kindness? What's one way our family could be like that helper this week?

Luke 2 – The Birth of Jesus

4. After visiting Jerusalem for Passover, Jesus was missing from His parents for three days as they traveled back home. How do you think His parents felt during that time?

   Parent/Adult Tip: This story is a great way to talk about the deep love and concern parents have for their children. Mary and Joseph experienced fear, worry, and confusion just like we would today if our child was missing. It's also an opportunity to help your children understand that even though Jesus was God's Son, He still had earthly parents who cared for Him deeply. Use this time to build connections by sharing personal stories or feelings about parenting, safety, and trust in God's plan.

   Ask: What would you do if you got separated from us for a whole day? What would you feel? Jesus said, *"Didn't you know that I would be in my Father's house?"* What do you think He meant? Can you imagine how hard it was for Mary and Joseph to raise God's Son? What would be hard about that? Parents, how would you feel if your child was missing for three days? How do we give our children the space to grow in their faith while still guiding and protecting them?

5. What can we learn from Jesus's example of wanting to be in *"His Father's house"*?

   Parent/Adult Tip: This moment from Jesus's childhood teaches us something powerful about how much He valued spending time with God and learning about His Father's will and Word. This is a great time to talk with your children about the importance of choosing to be near God regularly. *"His Father's house"* for us today can mean church, family devotion time, prayer, worship, or even quiet moments reading the Bible. Help your kids recognize that being in God's presence is not something we have to do; it's something we get to do. Talk to your children about what helps them feel close to God and what might make them feel distant. Share your own experience too.

Ask: Where do you feel closest to God? Is it church, bedtime prayers, or reading a Bible story? What are some ways we can be with God during our day? How do you feel about church or reading the Bible? Does church or reading the Bible help you grow or feel connected? Do we prioritize God's presence in our family schedule, or do other things crowd it out?

> *Closing Prayer:* Father, thank You for sending Your Son into the world. Help our family to make room in our hearts for Jesus every day. Let His light shine through us and help us keep each other accountable to prioritize Him every day as we grow together. In Jesus's name, we pray. Amen.

Day 3

Luke 3 – John Prepares the Way

Challenge: Can anyone say the memory verse without looking it up? Repeat the memory verse as a family.

Memory Verse of the Week: *"Nothing is impossible for God"* (Luke 1:37)!

Luke 3 – John Prepares the Way

> **Opening Prayer:** *God, as we read about John the Baptist, help us learn what it means to prepare our hearts for Jesus. Teach us to turn away from any wrong that we are doing and follow You. In Jesus's name, we pray. Amen.*

Luke 3:1-9 (GNT)

¹It was the fifteenth year of the rule of Emperor Tiberius; Pontius Pilate was governor of Judea, Herod was ruler of Galilee, and his brother Philip was ruler of the territory of Iturea and Trachonitis; Lysanias was ruler of Abilene, ² and Annas and Caiaphas were High Priests. At that time the word of God came to John son of Zechariah in the desert. ³ So John went throughout the whole territory of the Jordan River, preaching, "Turn away from your sins and be baptized, and God will forgive your sins." ⁴ As it is written in the book of the prophet Isaiah: "Someone is shouting in the desert: 'Get the road ready for the Lord; make a straight path for him to travel! ⁵ Every valley must be filled up, every hill and mountain leveled off. The winding roads must be made straight, and the rough paths made smooth.⁶ The whole human race will see God's salvation!'" ⁷ Crowds of people came out to John to be baptized by him. "You snakes!" he said to them. "Who told you that you could escape from the punishment God is about to send? ⁸ Do those things that will show that you have turned from your sins. And don't start saying among yourselves that Abraham is your ancestor. I tell you that God can take

these rocks and make descendants for Abraham! ⁹ The ax is ready to cut down the trees at the roots; every tree that does not bear good fruit will be cut down and thrown in the fire."

Fill in the blanks as a family before you continue:

- John the Baptist began preaching in the desert, telling people to _____ back to God and be _____ .

Answer: (turn, baptized)

- John's mission was to prepare the way for _____ , as the prophet _____ had written.

Answer: (Jesus, Isaiah)

- John called the people a "bunch of _____ " because they needed to show true repentance.

Answer: (snakes)

Luke 3:10-14 (GNT)

¹⁰ The people asked him, "What are we to do, then?" ¹¹ He answered, "Whoever has two shirts must give one to the man who has none, and whoever has food must share it." ¹² Some tax collectors came to be baptized, and they asked him, "Teacher, what are we to do?" ¹³ "Don't collect more than is legal," he told them. ¹⁴ Some soldiers also asked him, "What about us? What are we to do?" He said to them, "Don't take money from anyone by force or accuse anyone falsely. Be content with your pay."

Luke 3 – John Prepares the Way

Fill in the blanks as a family before you continue:

- When the crowd asked, "What should we do?" John told them to share their _____ and _____ with those in need.

   Answer: (food, shirts)

- John told tax collectors to not collect more from the people than is _____ .

   Answer: (legal)

Luke 3:15-22 (GNT)

¹⁵ People's hopes began to rise, and they began to wonder whether John perhaps might be the Messiah. ¹⁶ So John said to all of them, "I baptize you with water, but someone is coming who is much greater than I am. I am not good enough even to untie his sandals. He will baptize you with the Holy Spirit and fire. ¹⁷ He has his winnowing shovel with him, to thresh out all the grain and gather the wheat into his barn; but he will burn the chaff in a fire that never goes out." ¹⁸ In many different ways John preached the Good News to the people and urged them to change their ways. ¹⁹ But John reprimanded Governor Herod, because he had married Herodias, his brother's wife, and had done many other evil things. ²⁰ Then Herod did an even worse thing by putting John in prison. ²¹ After all the people had been baptized, Jesus also was baptized. While he was praying, heaven was opened, ²² and the Holy Spirit came down upon him in bodily form like a dove. And a voice came

from heaven, "You are my own dear Son. I am pleased with you."

Fill in the blanks as a family before you continue:

- The people wondered if _____ might be the _____ .

Answer: (John, Messiah)

- John said he baptizes with _____ , but the one coming after him will baptize with thevand with _____ .

Answer: (water, Holy Spirit, fire)

- Jesus Himself was _____ , and as He was praying, the _____ opened up.

Answer: (baptized, sky [heaven])

Luke 3:23-38 (GNT)

This section presents the genealogy of Jesus. If you want to stop here you can, or if you would like to read please go ahead. I have also attached a visual of Jesus's family tree that might be easier to read and pass around.

The Ancestors of Jesus

[23] When Jesus began his work, he was about thirty years old. He was the son, so people thought, of Joseph, who was the son of Heli, [24] the son of Matthat, the son of Levi, the son of Melchi, the son of Jannai, the son of Joseph, [25] the son of Mattathias, the son of Amos, the son of Nahum,

the son of Esli, the son of Naggai, ²⁶ the son of Maath, the son of Mattathias, the son of Semein, the son of Josech, the son of Joda, ²⁷ the son of Joanan, the son of Rhesa, the son of Zerubbabel, the son of Shealtiel, the son of Neri, ²⁸ the son of Melchi, the son of Addi, the son of Cosam, the son of Elmadam, the son of Er, ²⁹ the son of Joshua, the son of Eliezer, the son of Jorim, the son of Matthat, the son of Levi, ³⁰ the son of Simeon, the son of Judah, the son of Joseph, the son of Jonam, the son of Eliakim, ³¹ the son of Melea, the son of Menna, the son of Mattatha, the son of Nathan, the son of David, ³² the son of Jesse, the son of Obed, the son of Boaz, the son of Salmon, the son of Nahshon, ³³ the son of Amminadab, the son of Admin, the son of Arni, the son of Hezron, the son of Perez, the son of Judah, ³⁴ the son of Jacob, the son of Isaac, the son of Abraham, the son of Terah, the son of Nahor, ³⁵ the son of Serug, the son of Reu, the son of Peleg, the son of Eber, the son of Shelah, ³⁶ the son of Cainan, the son of Arphaxad, the son of Shem, the son of Noah, the son of Lamech, ³⁷ the son of Methuselah, the son of Enoch, the son of Jared, the son of Mahalaleel, the son of Kenan, ³⁸ the son of Enosh, the son of Seth, the son of Adam, the son of God.

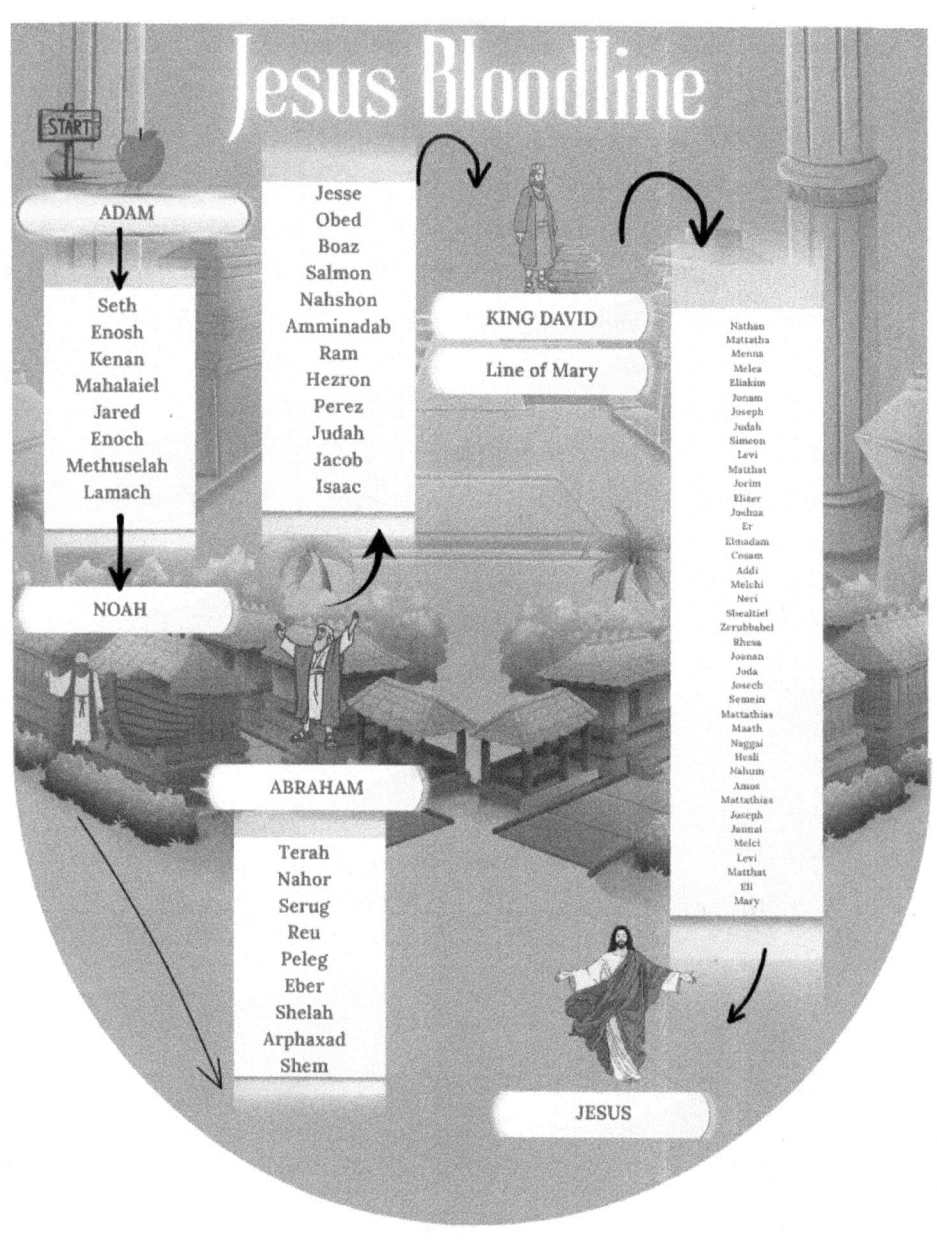

Luke 3 – John Prepares the Way

Family and Kid-Friendly Questions for Discussion

1. John's purpose in life was to "prepare the way" for Jesus. What does it mean to "prepare the way" for the Lord?

   Parent/Adult Tip: "Preparing the way" means getting our hearts ready to follow God, just like John the Baptist helped people do. He called them to turn away from sin, say sorry for the wrong things they had done, and choose to do what's right. That's still true for us today. As a Parent/Adult, you can help your children demonstrate repentance in their everyday lives by saying they're sorry when they do something wrong, making things right, and living in a way that honors God.

   Talk about how we can prepare our own hearts by being honest about sin, asking God to forgive us, and trying to live like Jesus. This is also a great time to reflect together as a family: Are we making room for Jesus in our home, our hearts, and our choices?

   Ask : If a king was coming to visit, what would we do to get ready? Would we clean up, decorate, prepare food? What's something you could ask God to help you do better today?

   John told people to turn from sin and live differently. What do you think that looks like for us today? What habits or distractions might be keeping us from drawing closer to God as a household? What are some ways we can turn our hearts back to God together as a family?

2. Why did John call people a bunch of snakes? What does it mean to "produce good fruit"?

    Parent/Adult Tip: John was bold because he wanted people to truly turn back to God, not just pretend. When he called them a "bunch of snakes," he meant they were being sneaky, pretending like they were good but not truly loving God in their hearts. As Parents/Adults, this is a chance to talk about the difference between doing the right thing just to look good versus doing it because we want to honor God. "Good fruit" means our actions show real faith, love, kindness, truth, and compassion.

    Ask: Why do you think John called the people snakes? Have you ever done something nice just to get a reward, but your heart didn't feel it? What could you do differently? Have you noticed someone who seemed to be faking kindness? Why do you think that matters to God? Parents/Adults, how do we model "good fruit" for our kids? What kind of "fruit" do we want our home to grow?

3. How can we practice kindness and fairness as John taught?

    Parent/Adult Tip: John encouraged people to share, be honest, and not take advantage of others. These are practical ways to love others and live out their faith. Talk with your children about real-life ways to treat others kindly and fairly at school, home, or in the neighborhood. Kids and teens learn best by seeing you live it out too.

    Ask: What's something you have that you could share with someone who needs it? Have you seen someone being treated unfairly? What could you do to help? Who can you be extra kind to this week even if it's hard? Make this a challenge! We all have someone in our lives who makes being kind difficult. How can you be an example of someone who follows Jesus by the way you treat others? Are we modeling kindness and fairness at home and in our community? Is there someone in our lives we can bless this week as a family?

4. How can we make God pleased with us like Jesus did? Give some examples.

    Parent/Adult Tip: God was pleased with Jesus not just because of what He did, but because Jesus lived a life fully surrendered to God's will. As we follow Jesus's example, showing love, forgiveness, obedience, and truth, we please God. Share stories with your children of moments when your actions honored God, and help them come up with examples of what that could look like this week.

    Ask: Can you think of something Jesus did that we could do too? How can you follow Jesus's example at home, at school, or with your friends? Jesus pleased God by obeying Him. What are some ways you can live that out this week? Is there something you've struggled with that you want God's help to change?

5. Why do you think the Bible includes the family tree of Jesus?

    Parent/Adult Tip: The genealogy of Jesus might seem like just a long list of names, but it shows that Jesus came from a real family in real history and that He fulfilled God's promises. This helps kids connect the dots to understand that Jesus's life isn't a made-up story. He had a family, a culture, and a mission that started long before He was born. It also helps kids understand that where they come from matters too.

Ask: Did you know Jesus had grandparents and great-grandparents, just like you? What does Jesus's family tree teach us about God's promises? Does knowing Jesus had real struggles, real family, and real relationships help you relate to Him more? Parent/Adults, how do we help our children understand their own value and identity in God's story? What can we do to show our family that we belong to Jesus's spiritual family too?

> **Closing Prayer:** *Thank You, Lord, for showing us how to live with hearts ready for You. Help our family walk in Your truth and grow in love like You did. Help our inside match our outside and help us not be deceitful like the Pharisees. We love You, Lord, and thank You for Your Word. In Your name, we pray. Amen.*

Day 4

Luke 4 – Jesus Says No to Temptation

Challenge: Can anyone say the memory verse without looking it up? Repeat the memory verse as a family.

Memory Verse of the Week: *"Nothing is impossible for God"* (Luke 1:37)!

Luke 4 – Jesus Says No to Temptation

> **Opening Prayer:** *Dear Father, as we read how Jesus faced temptation and began His ministry, help us learn to be strong like Him. Teach us to trust You when we feel weak and not let the enemy win our minds. We pray over every temptation that we will face and claim victory over them. In Jesus's name, we pray. Amen.*

Luke 4:1-15

¹ When Jesus returned from the Jordan River, the power of the Holy Spirit was with him, and the Spirit led him into the desert. ² For 40 days Jesus was tested by the devil, and during that time he went without eating. When it was all over, he was hungry. ³ The devil said to Jesus, "If you are God's Son, tell this stone to turn into bread." ⁴ Jesus answered, "The Scriptures say, 'No one can live only on food.'" ⁵ Then the devil led Jesus up to a high place and quickly showed him all the nations on earth. ⁶ The devil said, "I will give all this power and glory to you. It has been given to me, and I can give it to anyone I want. ⁷ Just worship me, and you can have it all." ⁸ Jesus answered, "The Scriptures say: 'Worship the Lord your God and serve only him!'" ⁹ Finally, the devil took Jesus to Jerusalem and had him stand on top of the temple. The devil said, "If you are God's Son, jump off. ¹⁰⁻¹¹ The Scriptures say: 'God will tell his angels to take care of you. They will catch you in their arms, and you will not hurt your feet on the stones.'" ¹² Jesus answered, "The Scriptures also say, 'Don't try to test the Lord your God!'" ¹³ After the devil had

finished testing Jesus in every way possible, he left him for a while. ¹⁴ Jesus returned to Galilee with the power of the Holy Spirit. News about him spread everywhere. ¹⁵ He taught in the Jewish synagogues, and everyone praised him.

Fill in the blanks as a family before you continue:

- Jesus was led by the _____ into the _____, where He was tempted by the devil for _____ days.

Answer: (devil, desert, 40)

- When the devil tempted Jesus to turn stones into bread, Jesus replied, "The Scriptures say, 'No one can live only on _____.'"

Answer: (food)

- After the temptation, Jesus returned to _____ with the power of the Holy Spirit, and news about Him spread _____.

Answer: (Galilee, everywhere)

Luke 4:16-30

¹⁶ Jesus went back to Nazareth, where he had been brought up, and as usual, he went to the synagogue on the Sabbath. When he stood up to read from the Scriptures, ¹⁷ he was given the book of Isaiah the prophet. He opened it and read, ¹⁸ "The Lord's Spirit has come to me, because he has chosen me to tell the good news to the poor. The Lord has sent me to announce freedom for prisoners, to give sight to the blind, to free everyone who suffers, ¹⁹ and to say, 'This is the

Luke 4 – Jesus Says No to Temptation

year the Lord has chosen.'" [20] Jesus closed the book, then handed it back to the man in charge and sat down. Everyone in the synagogue looked straight at Jesus.[21] Then Jesus said to them, "What you have just heard me read has come true today." [22] All the people started talking about Jesus and were amazed at the wonderful things he said. They kept on asking, "Isn't he Joseph's son?" [23] Jesus answered: You will certainly want to tell me this saying, "Doctor, first make yourself well." You will tell me to do the same things here in your own hometown that you heard I did in Capernaum. [24] But you can be sure that no prophets are liked by the people of their own hometown. [25] Once during the time of Elijah, there was no rain for three and a half years, and people everywhere were starving. [26] There were many widows in Israel, but Elijah was sent only to a widow in the town of Zarephath, near the city of Sidon. [27] During the time of the prophet Elisha, many men in Israel had leprosy, but no one was healed, except Naaman who lived in Syria. [28] When the people in the synagogue heard Jesus say this, they became so angry [29] that they got up and threw him out of town. They dragged him to the edge of the cliff on which the town was built, because they wanted to throw him down from there. [30] But Jesus slipped through the crowd and got away.

Fill in the blanks as a family before you continue:

- In the synagogue of _____ , Jesus read from the scroll of the prophet _____ , declaring, "The Lord's Spirit has come to me . . . ," and said that the Scripture had been fulfilled that day.

Answer: (Nazareth, Isaiah)

- The people became angry when Jesus said that no prophet is accepted in his _____ , and they attempted to throw Him off a _____ , but He passed through the crowd and went on His way.

    Answer: (hometown, cliff)

Luke 4:31-44

⁣³¹ Jesus went to the town of Capernaum in Galilee and taught the people on the Sabbath. ³² They were surprised at the things he taught, because he spoke with power. ³³ There in the Jewish meeting place was a man with an evil spirit. He yelled out, ³⁴ "Hey, Jesus of Nazareth! What do you want with us? Are you here to destroy us? I know who you are! You are God's Holy One." ³⁵ Jesus ordered the evil spirit to be quiet and come out. The demon threw the man to the ground in front of everyone and left without harming him. ³⁶ They all were amazed and kept saying to each other, "What kind of teaching is this? He has power to order evil spirits out, and they obey him!" ³⁷ News about Jesus spread all over that part of the country.

³⁸ Jesus left the synagogue and went to Simon's home. When Jesus got there, he was told that Simon's mother-in-law was sick with a high fever. ³⁹ So Jesus went over to her and ordered the fever to go away. Right then she was able to get up and serve them a meal. ⁴⁰ After the sun had set, people with all kinds of diseases were brought to Jesus. He put his hands on each one of them and healed them. ⁴¹ Demons went out of many people and shouted, "You are the Son of God!" But

Luke 4 – Jesus Says No to Temptation

Jesus ordered the demons not to speak because they knew he was the Messiah. ⁴² The next morning Jesus went out to a place where he could be alone, and the crowds looked for him. When they found him, they tried to stop him from leaving. ⁴³ But Jesus said, "People in other towns must hear the good news about God's kingdom. That's why I was sent." ⁴⁴ So he kept on preaching in the Jewish synagogues in Judea.

Fill in the blanks as a family before you continue:

- Jesus ordered the evil spirit to _____ , and it came out without doing the man any harm.

    Answer: (be quiet)

- Jesus said that He had to tell the good news about _____ in other towns also. That is what God sent Him to do.

    Answer: (God's Kingdom)

Family and Kid-Friendly Questions for Discussion

1. How do you think the people felt when they saw Jesus tell the evil spirit to leave the man? What does this story teach us about trusting Jesus when we're scared?

    Parent/Adult Tip: Most of the people were amazed, maybe even shocked or scared because they had never seen someone with that kind of power. This moment showed Jesus had authority over even the scariest things. Kids (and adults) need to be reminded that Jesus is bigger than anything we're afraid of. He's our protector and is always in control.

Ask: How would you have felt if you were there? Have you ever been afraid of something? What helped you feel better? What does trusting Jesus when you're scared look like in your life? Parents/Adults, how do we help our kids understand that Jesus is with them even in scary moments, even when it feels like He's not there? As a family, let's each share one fear we've had and then pray together, asking Jesus to give us peace.

2. Why do you think Jesus cared about helping Simon's mother-in-law?

   Parent/Adult Tip: Jesus didn't only do big miracles; He also cared about everyday struggles. He helped Simon's mother-in-law because He cared deeply for each person, not just crowds. Use this moment to show kids that Jesus cares when anyone is hurting, (for example, when someone is sick or having anxiety); this includes people in our family or friend groups. He loves us and wants to meet every need we have, big or small.

   Ask: Have you ever prayed for someone who was sick? What happened? Do you believe Jesus cares about even the small things in your life? Why or why not? What is something small that you think Jesus does not care about? When have we seen God answer a prayer for healing in our family or community? Ask each family member to share the name of one person we can pray for, someone who is sick or going through a hard time right now.

   Challenge: Take three minutes to write down a prayer for that person. If you are comfortable doing so, give them your written prayer tomorrow.

3. Why was it important for Jesus to tell others about God's Kingdom?

   Parent/Adult Tip: Jesus came to share the most important news, the best news—that God loves us, forgives us, and wants us to live forever with Him. He didn't keep that message to Himself; He invited people into God's family. Kids and teens can understand the value of sharing good news with others. Remind them that we can share God's love through our words and our actions. My pastor says, "Some people will never open the Bible; you might be the only Bible they encounter."

   Ask: What's one way you can show kindness or share about God this week? Do you ever feel nervous sharing about Jesus? What could help make that easier? Parents/Adults, how are we modeling a life that shows others what God's Kingdom is like?

4. Why do you think Jesus didn't give in to temptation when He was tired and hungry?

   Parent/Adult Tip: Temptation can come when we're tired, stressed, or hungry, just like it did for Jesus. I love the Bible because Jesus is giving us examples and tools to follow. If Jesus was tempted, that means we will be tempted too. Help your children understand that being tempted isn't a sin, but giving in is. Jesus gave us the perfect example of how to respond: He used Scripture and trusted God. Teach your kids to memorize Bible verses to help them when they face peer pressure, frustration, or tough choices.

Bible Verses for Temptation and Peer Pressure

- **1 Corinthians 10:13:** *"You are tempted in the same way that everyone else is tempted. But God can be trusted not to let you be tempted too much, and he will show you how to escape from your temptations."*

    Why it helps: This reminds us that we are not alone and that God always provides a way out of temptation.

- **James 4:7:** *"Surrender to God! Resist the devil, and he will run from you."*

    Why it helps: You can say no to wrong things when you choose to follow God. Evil has to flee when we choose God over temptation.

- **Psalm 119:11:** *"I treasure your word above all else; it keeps me from sinning against you."*

    Why it helps: God's Word gives us strength and wisdom to choose what's right, even when it's hard.

- **Proverbs 1:10:** *"Don't be tempted by sinners or listen when they say, 'Come on!'"*

    Why it helps: Peer pressure is real, but this verse reminds us to stay strong and not follow others into bad choices.

- **Galatians 1:10:** *"I am not trying to please people. I want to please God. If I were doing that, I would not be a servant of Christ."*

    Why it helps: This verse gives confidence to stand up for what's right, even if it's unpopular.

Ask: What are some things that are hard to say no to, even when we know we should? (For example, this could include unhealthy food or drugs or bullying.) What kind of temptations do you face at school or online? How can God's Word help? Parent/Adults, how do we model resisting temptation in our daily life?

5. Why do you think the people in Jesus's hometown didn't like what He said? Have you ever felt left out or rejected?

Parent/Adult Tip: I love this story because this is a perfect example for anyone who is new in their walk with Christ to read. When I came to faith in Christ, I knew that some of my family and friends would be the first to call out my past mistakes and make me feel like I was not good enough in my walk with Christ. This could be the same for kids and their peers. Familiarity can make it hard to grow, and rejection can hurt, especially when it comes from the people we expect to support us. Jesus understands that pain. Helping kids know that even Jesus wasn't always accepted gives them comfort when they feel left out or misunderstood. Remind them that their identity is in God, not in the opinions of others and that sometimes, we need to move on even when rejection hurts just like Jesus did.

Ask: Has someone refused to be your friend or made you feel left out? How did you feel? What helps you keep your confidence when people don't accept you or your faith? What can we do as a family to support each other when we feel rejected? How can we remember that God always loves and accepts us, even when others don't?

> **Closing Prayer:** *Heavenly Father, thank You for Jesus's example of courage and strength. Thank you for showing us exactly how to handle temptations from the devil with Your Word. Help us grow in our knowledge of the Scripture and know how to apply it in any situation. Help our family stand firm in our faith and share Your good news with others. In Jesus's name, we pray. Amen.*

Day 5

Luke 5 - Jesus Chooses His Helpers

Challenge: Can anyone say the memory verse without looking it up? Repeat the memory verse as a family.

Memory Verse of the Week: *"Nothing is impossible for God"* (Luke 1:37)!

> **Opening Prayer:** *Heavenly Father, help us listen closely to the stories of healing, calling, and forgiveness. Open our eyes and hearts to see how You call each of us to follow You. In Jesus's name, we pray. Amen.*

Luke 5 – Jesus Chooses His Helpers

Luke 5:1-11 (GNT)

¹ One day Jesus was standing on the shore of Lake Gennesaret while the people pushed their way up to him to listen to the word of God. ² He saw two boats pulled up on the beach; the fishermen had left them and were washing the nets. ³ Jesus got into one of the boats—it belonged to Simon—and asked him to push off a little from the shore. Jesus sat in the boat and taught the crowd. ⁴ When he finished speaking, he said to Simon, "Push the boat out further to the deep water, and you and your partners let down your nets for a catch." ⁵ "Master," Simon answered, "we worked hard all night long and caught nothing. But if you say so, I will let down the nets." ⁶ They let them down and caught such a large number of fish that the nets were about to break. ⁷ So they motioned to their partners in the other boat to come and help them. They came and filled both boats so full of fish that the boats were about to sink. ⁸ When Simon Peter saw what had happened, he fell on his knees before Jesus and said, "Go away from me, Lord! I am a sinful man!" ⁹ He and the others with him were all amazed at the large number of fish they had caught. ¹⁰ The same was true of Simon's partners, James and John, the sons of Zebedee. Jesus said to Simon, "Don't be afraid; from now on you will be catching people." ¹¹ They pulled the boats up on the beach, left everything, and followed Jesus.

Fill in the blanks as a family before you continue:

- Jesus was teaching by a _____ when He told Simon to let down his _____ after a night of catching nothing. Simon obeyed, and they caught so many _____ that their nets began to break.

  Answer: (lake, nets, fish)

- Jesus told Simon not to be afraid, because from then on, he would fish for _____ . Simon and his partners left everything and followed _____ .

  Answer: (people, Jesus)

Luke 5:12-16 (GNT)

[12] Once Jesus was in a town where there was a man who was suffering from a dreaded skin disease. When he saw Jesus, he threw himself down and begged him, "Sir, if you want to, you can make me clean!" [13] Jesus reached out and touched him. "I do want to," he answered. "Be clean!" At once the disease left the man. [14] Jesus ordered him, "Don't tell anyone, but go straight to the priest and let him examine you; then to prove to everyone that you are cured, offer the sacrifice as Moses ordered." [15] But the news about Jesus spread all the more widely, and crowds of people came to hear him and be healed from their diseases. [16] But he would go away to lonely places, where he prayed.

Luke 5 – Jesus Chooses His Helpers

Fill in the blanks as a family before you continue:

- A man with a dreaded skin _____ begged Jesus to make him _____. Jesus, filled with compassion, touched him and _____ him; then Jesus told him not to tell _____.

Answer: (disease, clean, healed, anyone)

Luke 5:17-32 (GNT)

¹⁷ One day when Jesus was teaching, some Pharisees and teachers of the Law were sitting there who had come from every town in Galilee and Judea and from Jerusalem. The power of the Lord was present for Jesus to heal the sick. ¹⁸ Some men came carrying a paralyzed man on a bed, and they tried to carry him into the house and put him in front of Jesus. ¹⁹ Because of the crowd, however, they could find no way to take him in. So they carried him up on the roof, made an opening in the tiles, and let him down on his bed into the middle of the group in front of Jesus. ²⁰ When Jesus saw how much faith they had, he said to the man, "Your sins are forgiven, my friend." ²¹ The teachers of the Law and the Pharisees began to say to themselves, "Who is this man who speaks such blasphemy! God is the only one who can forgive sins!" ²² Jesus knew their thoughts and said to them, "Why do you think such things? ²³ Is it easier to say, 'Your sins are forgiven you,' or to say, 'Get up and walk'? ²⁴ I will prove to you, then, that the Son of Man has authority on earth to forgive sins." So he said to the paralyzed man, "I tell you, get up, pick up your bed, and go home!"²⁵ At once

the man got up in front of them all, took the bed he had been lying on, and went home, praising God. ²⁶ They were all completely amazed! Full of fear, they praised God, saying, "What marvelous things we have seen today!" ²⁷ After this, Jesus went out and saw a tax collector named Levi, sitting in his office. Jesus said to him, "Follow me." ²⁸ Levi got up, left everything, and followed him.²⁹ Then Levi had a big feast in his house for Jesus, and among the guests was a large number of tax collectors and other people. ³⁰ Some Pharisees and some teachers of the Law who belonged to their group complained to Jesus' disciples. "Why do you eat and drink with tax collectors and other outcasts?" they asked. ³¹ Jesus answered them, "People who are well do not need a doctor, but only those who are sick. ³² I have not come to call respectable people to repent, but outcasts."

Fill in the blanks as a family before you continue:

- Jesus can _____ sin. When friends lowered a _____ man through the roof, Jesus _____ him and forgave his sins, showing God's power.

    Answer: (forgive, paralyzed, healed)

- Jesus came to help sinners. When people asked why Jesus ate with _____ , He said He came to invite them to turn back to _____ .

    Answers: (outcasts, God)

Luke 5 – Jesus Chooses His Helpers

Luke 5:33-39 (GNT)

> ³³ Some people said to Jesus, "The disciples of John fast frequently and offer prayers, and the disciples of the Pharisees do the same; but your disciples eat and drink." ³⁴ Jesus answered, "Do you think you can make the guests at a wedding party go without food as long as the bridegroom is with them? Of course not! ³⁵ But the day will come when the bridegroom will be taken away from them, and then they will fast." ³⁶ Jesus also told them this parable: "You don't tear a piece off a new coat to patch up an old coat. If you do, you will have torn the new coat, and the piece of new cloth will not match the old. ³⁷ Nor do you pour new wine into used wineskins, because the new wine will burst the skins, the wine will pour out, and the skins will be ruined. ³⁸ Instead, new wine must be poured into fresh wineskins! ³⁹ And you don't want new wine after drinking old wine. 'The old is better,' you say."

Fill in the blanks as a family before you continue:

- Jesus said the time would come when He would be taken from His disciples, and then they would _____ .

Answer: (fast)

- New things, like the gospel, can't fit into old ways, just like _____ wine can't be put into used wineskins.

Answer: (new)

Family and Kid-Friendly Questions for Discussion

1. Why do you think Simon Peter decided to obey Jesus even though he hadn't caught any fish all night?

   Parent/Adult Tip: Sometimes, our kids (and we Parents/Adults) are asked to trust God even when things don't make sense or situations feel discouraging. This passage about Simon Peter is a great example of what can happen when we trust Jesus beyond logic or feelings. Remind your children that obedience often comes before blessings; we don't always see the "big catch" right away. This is a good time to talk about obedience. We don't hear God just by listening; we have to read His Word and spend quality time with Him to hear what He wants us to do. Spending time with Him is the first step to obedience.

   Ask: Parents/Adults, share a time when you obeyed God even though it was hard or confusing (e.g., in tithing or sickness). What happened? Kids, have you ever done something good just because a trusted adult or Jesus said to? What was the result?

2. How do you think the man with leprosy (i.e., "the dreaded skin disease") felt when Jesus touched and healed him?

   Parent/Adult Tip: Use this teaching to talk about compassion. In Jesus's time, lepers were outcasts, and treated poorly, but Jesus touched the leper before healing him. That touch showed love when no one else would come near the man. This teaches us how important kindness and compassion are, especially to those others might ignore.

   Ask: Parents/Adults, how can we model kindness to people who feel left out or different? Can you think of someone at school or in your neighborhood who might feel alone? What can you do this week to show them Jesus's love?

3. Why do you think the paralyzed man's friends worked so hard to bring him to Jesus?

   Parent/Adult Tip: This is an awesome story about friendship and faith. The man's friends didn't give up; they knew Jesus could help, so they found a creative way to get their friend to Him. Talk about friendships with your kids and ask them if their friends are bringing them closer to God or drawing them further away. It matters who we surround ourselves with. If this paralyzed man had different friends, he might have been paralyzed forever, but because he surrounded himself with people of faith in God, he was healed.

   Ask: Who are your closest friends? Are they bringing you closer to God or drawing you further away? What kind of friend are you? It's okay to be honest at this moment; we want to grow. Are you bringing your friends closer to Christ or drawing them further away? How can we be bold in our faith just as this man's friends were? What could have happened to the man if he hadn't had them as friends? (Talk about how important it is to make good decisions about the people we choose to surround ourselves with.) Is there a friend or family member you can pray for, talk to about Jesus, or help this week? What could that look like?

4. Why did Jesus choose to eat with tax collectors and outcasts (i.e., sinners) instead of the "respectable" people?

   Parent/Adult Tip: This is a great time to talk about how Jesus sees value in everyone, especially those others might judge wrongly.

Tax collectors were considered dishonest and "bad" back then, but Jesus loved them and wanted to help them change. Help your kids understand that Jesus doesn't wait for people to be perfect; He meets them where they are. We are all imperfect, and I thank God that He wants to save and change us. As a family, this is a chance to reflect on showing kindness to others, even those who may not make good choices yet.

Ask: Parent/Adults, talk about a time when you showed kindness to someone that others didn't treat kindly. Why did you do it? Kids, have you ever chosen to include someone that others left out or called "bad"? How did that feel? What do you think Jesus wants us to do when we see someone who is different or who has made mistakes?

> **Closing Prayer:** *Lord, thank You for calling ordinary people to do great things for You. Help our family to say yes when You call and to show Your love every day. Lord, surround us with people who love You and who would take us up to the roof just to see You. In Your name, we pray. Amen.*

Day 6

Luke 6 – Jesus Teaches about Love

Challenge: Can anyone say the memory verse without looking it up? Repeat the memory verse as a family.

Memory Verse of the Week: *"Nothing is impossible for God"* (Luke 1:37)!

> **Opening Prayer:** *God, help us understand how Jesus wants us to live. As we read His teachings today, give our family hearts ready to forgive, love, and follow Him. We thank You for such an amazing example. In Jesus's name, we pray. Amen.*

Luke 6:1-11

¹ One Sabbath when Jesus and his disciples were walking through some wheat fields, the disciples picked some wheat. They rubbed the husks off with their hands and started eating the grain. ² Some Pharisees said, "Why are you picking grain on the Sabbath? You're not supposed to do that!" ³ Jesus answered, "You surely have read what David did when he and his followers were hungry. ⁴ He went into the house of God and took the sacred loaves of bread that only the priests supposed to eat it. He not only ate some himself, but even gave some to his followers." ⁵ Jesus finished by saying, "The Son of Man is Lord of the Sabbath."

⁶ On another Sabbath, Jesus was teaching in a synagogue, and a man with a paralyzed right hand was there. ⁷ Some Pharisees and teachers of the Law of Moses kept watching Jesus to see if he would heal the man. They did this because they wanted to accuse Jesus of doing something wrong. ⁸ Jesus knew what they were thinking, so he told the man to stand up where everyone could see him. And the man stood up. ⁹ Then Jesus asked, "On the Sabbath, should we do good deeds or evil deeds? Should we save someone's life or destroy it?" ¹⁰ After he had looked around at everyone, he told the man, "Stretch out your hand." He did, and his hand became completely well. ¹¹ The teachers and the Pharisees were furious and started saying to one another, "What can we do about Jesus?"

Fill in the blanks as a family before you continue:

- Jesus reminded the Pharisees that _____ and his men ate the special bread when they were hungry, even though it was only for priests.

  Answer: (David)

- Jesus said that "the Son of Man is _____ over the Sabbath," meaning He has power over the Sabbath.

  Answer: (Lord)

- The Pharisees watched Jesus closely to see if He would _____ on the Sabbath, so they could accuse Him.

  Answer: (heal)

Luke 6 – Jesus Teaches about Love

Luke 6:12-26

¹² About that time Jesus went off to a mountain to pray, and he spent the whole night there. ¹³ The next morning he called his disciples together and chose twelve of them to be his apostles. ¹⁴ One was Simon, and Jesus named him Peter. Another was Andrew, Peter's brother. There was also James, John, Philip, Bartholomew, ¹⁵ Matthew, Thomas, and James the son of Alphaeus. The rest of the apostles were Simon, known as the Eager One, ¹⁶ Jude, who was the son of James, and Judas Iscariot, who later betrayed Jesus. ¹⁷ Jesus and his apostles went down from the mountain and came to some flat, level ground. Many other disciples were there to meet him. Large crowds of people from all over Judea, Jerusalem, and the coastal towns of Tyre and Sidon were there too. ¹⁸ These people had come to listen to Jesus and to be healed of their diseases. All who were troubled by evil spirits were also healed. ¹⁹ Everyone was trying to touch Jesus, because power was going out from him and healing them all.

²⁰ Jesus looked at his disciples and said: God will bless you people who are poor. His kingdom belongs to you! ²¹ God will bless you hungry people. You will have plenty to eat! God will bless you people who are now crying. You will laugh! ²² God will bless you when others hate you and won't have anything to do with you. God will bless you when people insult you and say cruel things about you, all because you are a follower of the Son of Man. ²³ Long ago your own people did these same things to the prophets. So when this happens to you, be happy and jump for joy! You will have

a great reward in heaven. ²⁴ But you rich people are in for trouble. You have already had an easy life! ²⁵ You well-fed people are in for trouble. You will go hungry! You people who are laughing now are in for trouble. You are going to cry and weep! ²⁶ You are in for trouble when everyone says good things about you. That is what your own people said about those prophets who told lies.

Fill in the blanks as a family before you continue:

- Jesus went up on a mountain to _____ all night before choosing His twelve apostles.

Answer: (pray)

- Jesus chose twelve men to be His _____ who would follow Him and spread His teachings.

Answer: (apostles)

- Jesus said that God would bless people who are _____ because His kingdom belongs to them.

Answer: (poor)

Luke 6:27-42

²⁷ This is what I say to all who will listen to me: Love your enemies, and be good to everyone who hates you. ²⁸ Ask God to bless those who curse you and pray for everyone who is cruel to you. ²⁹ If someone slaps you on one cheek, don't stop that person from slapping you on the other cheek. If someone wants to take your coat, don't try to keep back your

shirt. ³⁰ Give to everyone who asks and don't ask people to return what they have taken from you. ³¹ Treat others just as you want to be treated. ³² If you love only someone who loves you, will God praise you for that? ³³ If you are kind only to someone who is kind to you, will God be pleased with you for that? Even sinners are kind to people who are kind to them. ³⁴ If you lend money only to someone you think will pay you back, will God be pleased with you for that? Even sinners lend to sinners because they think they will get it back. ³⁵ But love your enemies and be good to them. Lend without expecting to be paid back. Then you will get a great reward, and you will be the true children of God in heaven. He is good even to people who are unthankful and cruel. ³⁶ Have pity on others just as your Father has pity on you.

³⁷ Don't judge others, and God won't judge you. Don't be hard on others, God won't be hard on you. Forgive others, and God will forgive you. ³⁸ If you give to others, you will be given a full amount in return. It will be packed down, shaken together, and spilling over into your lap. The way you treat others is the way you will be treated." ³⁹ Jesus also used some sayings as he spoke to the people. He said: Can one blind person lead another blind person? Won't they both fall into a ditch? ⁴⁰ Are students better than their teacher? But when they are fully trained, they will be like their teacher. ⁴¹ You can see the speck in your friend's eye, but you don't notice the log in your eye. ⁴² How can you say, "My friend, let me take the speck out of your eye," when you don't see the log in your own eye? You show-offs! First, get the log out of your own eye; then you can see how to take the speck out of your friend's eye.

Fill in the blanks as a family before you continue:

- Jesus taught, "Love your _____ , and be good to everyone who hates you."

  Answer: (enemies)

- Jesus taught that you should treat others as you want them to be _____ .

  Answer: (treated)

- Jesus taught that instead of judging others, we should first fix our own _____ before correcting someone else.

  Answer: (faults)

Luke 6:43-49

⁴³ A good tree cannot produce bad fruit, and a bad tree cannot produce good fruit. ⁴⁴ You can tell what a tree is like by the fruit it produces. You cannot pick figs or grapes from thornbushes. ⁴⁵ Good people do good things because of the good in their hearts, but bad people do bad things because of the evil in their hearts. Your words show what is in your heart. ⁴⁶ Why do you keep on saying that I am your Lord when you refuse to do what I say? ⁴⁷ Anyone who comes to me and obeys me ⁴⁸ is like someone who dug down deep and built a house on solid rock. When a flood came and the river rushed against the house, it was built so well that it didn't even shake. ⁴⁹ But anyone who hears what I say and doesn't obey me is like someone whose house wasn't built on solid rock. As soon as the river rushed against the house, it was smashed to pieces!

Luke 6 – Jesus Teaches about Love

Fill in the blanks as a family before you continue:

- Jesus said that a good tree produces _____ fruit, and a bad tree produces bad fruit.

    Answer: (good)

- Jesus compared a person who listens to His words and follows them to someone who builds their house on a _____ foundation.

    Answer: (rock or strong)

Family and Kid-Friendly Questions for Discussion

1. Why did Jesus heal on the Sabbath even though some people didn't like it?

    Parent/Adult Tip: This lesson teaches that God's love is bigger than religious rules. Sometimes, we need to choose kindness over tradition. Let your child know that doing what's right is not always popular, but it is always worth it in God's eyes. Model this with small choices at home.

    Ask: Why do you think Jesus helped someone even though people were watching and judging Him? Have you ever helped someone even when others didn't? What's more important: following rules or helping someone who is hurting?

2. Why did Jesus choose ordinary people to be His disciples?

    Parent/Adult Tip: Remind your children that God doesn't look for "perfect" people; He chooses people with willing hearts. Let your children know they don't have to be the smartest, fastest, or most popular to be used by God. Encourage them in their unique gifts and purpose. This is a good time to discuss their gifts and how their gifts can be used for God's kingdom.

Ask: Do you think Jesus would choose you to follow Him? Why or why not? Were Jesus's disciples perfect people? Did they have flaws? What do you think God loves about how He made you? How can you serve or follow God in your everyday life?

3. What did Jesus mean when He said, "Love your enemies"?

   Parent/Adult Tip: This one is tough even for grown-ups, especially for grow-ups! Teach your children that love isn't always about liking someone; it's about choosing kindness and forgiveness even when someone is mean. You're showing Jesus through your heart and actions, which is hard to do, sometimes. This is a great time to discuss hard situations such as cyber bullying and kids in school that can be unkind.

   Ask: Has anyone been unkind to you? How did you respond? What would it look like to "love" someone who hurt your feelings? Why do you think Jesus wants us to do this?

4. Why does Jesus say we're not to judge others?

   Parent/Adult Tip: Judging others can feel easy, but it can also hurt relationships. Help your child understand how it feels to be judged and how grace and understanding can heal. We have all made mistakes and done something we are not proud of; this is a great time to discuss how we want to be treated in those moments. We need to remember that none of us is perfect; therefore, we need to show compassion to others when they make mistakes. Reflect on how God shows us grace, even when we mess up.

Ask: Have you ever been judged unfairly or misunderstood? How did it feel? What can you do if you notice yourself being too harsh with someone? How can we show God's love instead of judgment?

5. What does it mean to forgive others like God forgives us?

    Parent/Adult Tip: We can struggle with forgiveness, especially when someone doesn't say sorry. Help children see that forgiveness is more for their heart than for the other person. Share a story of when you forgave someone and how it brought peace; also share about times when you didn't forgive and how that affected you. Forgiveness is not easy at all, but thank God we have a God who loves us and sets an amazing example of how to forgive.

    Ask: Is it easier to forgive someone who says sorry or someone who doesn't? Why? Is there anyone who has hurt you—someone you need to forgive? How does forgiving help your heart feel better? How many times does Jesus say to forgive someone? Does this mean that if we have forgiven someone, we need to stay in the same situation (e.g., continue a relationship with a friend who continually hurts you or is mean to you)?

6. Why does Jesus talk about building a house on rock versus building a house on something other than solid rock (sand)?

   Parent/Adult Tip: This story is a picture of what happens when we build our lives on truth. Help your child see that trusting Jesus gives strength in tough times. We are to stand firm in God's Word, continually build our faith, and focus on God; by doing so, we will be building our "house" on His rock. Then when tough times come, we won't fall apart like sand, but stand firm and strong because we are trusting in God's Word.

   Ask: What are some "rocks" in your life—things that make you strong? What's something that could be like "sand" that might not last? How can we make our family stronger in our faith?

7. Why does Jesus care so much about how we treat others?

   Parent/Adult Tip: Jesus said that the greatest commandments are to love God and love others. If we love God but treat others badly, we're missing the point. Talk as a family about kindness being part of worship.

   Ask: How can you treat your family with more love this week? How can you treat people who aren't so kind to you with love this week? This could be as simple as not participating in the gossip and drama that about them. Sometimes, closing our mouths is a way of showing kindness. What would someone learn about Jesus just by watching how you treat people? Have you ever failed to treat someone kindly? What could you have done better?

Closing Prayer: *Thank You, God, for the wisdom of Jesus. Help our family live by His words, love our enemies, and treat others the way we want to be treated. Lord, we want to bear "good fruit" and not just put on a show; we want to be transformed from the inside out. In Jesus's name, we pray. Amen.*

Day 7

Luke 7 – Jesus Helps and Heals

Challenge: Can anyone say the memory verse without looking it up? Repeat the memory verse as a family.

Memory Verse of the Week: *"Nothing is impossible for God"* (Luke 1:37)!

Opening Prayer: *Heavenly Father, open our hearts to see the faith of the people in today's chapter of the Gospel of Luke. Help us to trust You with every need and show compassion to everyone, even when it's hard, like Jesus did. We thank You, Lord, for being such a great father and example. In Jesus's name, we pray. Amen.*

Luke 7:1-16 (GNT)

¹When Jesus had finished saying all these things to the people, he went to Capernaum. ² A Roman officer there had a servant who was very dear to him; the man was sick and about to die. ³ When the officer heard about Jesus, he sent some Jewish elders to ask him to come and heal his servant. ⁴ They came to Jesus and begged him earnestly, "This man really deserves your help. ⁵ He loves our people and he himself built a synagogue for us." ⁶ So Jesus went with them. He was not far from the house when the officer sent friends to tell him, "Sir, don't trouble yourself. I do not deserve to have you come into my house, ⁷ neither do I consider myself worthy to come to you in person. Just give the order, and my servant will get well. ⁸ I, too, am a man placed under the authority of superior officers, and I have soldiers under me. I order this one, 'Go!' and he goes; I order that one, 'Come!' and he comes; and I order my slave, 'Do this!' and he does it." ⁹ Jesus was surprised when he heard this; he turned around and said to the crowd following him, "I tell you, I have never found faith like this, not even in Israel!" ¹⁰ The messengers went back to the officer's house and found his servant well.

¹¹ Soon afterward Jesus went to a town named Nain, accompanied by his disciples and a large crowd. ¹² Just as he arrived at the gate of the town, a funeral procession was coming out. The dead man was the only son of a woman who was a widow, and a large crowd from the town was with her. ¹³ When the Lord saw her, his heart was filled with pity for her, and he said to her, "Don't cry." ¹⁴ Then he

Luke 7 – Jesus Helps and Heals

walked over and touched the coffin, and the men carrying it stopped. Jesus said, "Young man! Get up, I tell you!" ¹⁵ The dead man sat up and began to talk, and Jesus gave him back to his mother. ¹⁶ They all were filled with fear and praised God. "A great prophet has appeared among us!" they said; "God has come to save his people!"

Fill in the blanks as a family before you continue:

- When the Roman officer heard about Jesus, he sent some Jewish leaders to ask Jesus to come and _____ his servant.

  Answer: (heal)

- The officer sent messengers to Jesus to say that he was not worthy and that if He would just speak, the man's servant would be healed. Jesus said, "I have never found _____ like this even in Israel!"

  Answer: (faith)

- The people said, "A great _____ has appeared among us," and "God has come to save his people."

  Answer: (prophet)

Luke 7:17-29 (GNT)

¹⁷ This news about Jesus went out through all the country and the surrounding territory. ¹⁸ When John's disciples told him about all these things, he called two of them ¹⁹ and sent them to the Lord to ask him, "Are you the one John said was

going to come, or should we expect someone else?" ²⁰ When they came to Jesus, they said, "John the Baptist sent us to ask if you are the one he said was going to come, or should we expect someone else?" ²¹ At that very time Jesus healed many people from their sicknesses, diseases, and evil spirits, and gave sight to many blind people. ²² He answered John's messengers, "Go back and tell John what you have seen and heard: the blind can see, the lame can walk, those who suffer from dreaded skin diseases are made clean, the deaf can hear, the dead are raised to life, and the Good News is preached to the poor. ²³ How happy are those who have no doubts about me!" ²⁴ After John's messengers had left, Jesus began to speak about him to the crowds: "When you went out to John in the desert, what did you expect to see? A blade of grass bending in the wind? ²⁵ What did you go out to see? A man dressed up in fancy clothes? People who dress like that and live in luxury are found in palaces! ²⁶ Tell me, what did you go out to see? A prophet? Yes indeed, but you saw much more than a prophet. ²⁷ For John is the one of whom the scripture says: 'God said, I will send my messenger ahead of you to open the way for you.' ²⁸ I tell you," Jesus added, "John is greater than anyone who has ever lived. But the one who is least in the Kingdom of God is greater than John." ²⁹ All the people heard him; they and especially the tax collectors were the ones who had obeyed God's righteous demands and had been baptized by John.

Luke 7 – Jesus Helps and Heals

Fill in the blanks as a family before you continue:

- John's disciples told him about all these things. So John called two of them and sent them to the _____ to ask, "Are you the one John said was going to come, or should we _____ someone else?"

Answer: (Lord, expect)

- "I tell you," Jesus added, _____ is greater than anyone who has ever lived. But the one who is least in the Kingdom of God is greater than John."

Answer: (John)

Luke 7:30-48 (GNT)

[30] But the Pharisees and the teachers of the Law rejected God's purpose for themselves and refused to be baptized by John. [31] Jesus continued, "Now to what can I compare the people of this day? What are they like? [32] They are like children sitting in the marketplace. One group shouts to the other, 'We played wedding music for you, but you wouldn't dance! We sang funeral songs, but you wouldn't cry!' [33] John the Baptist came, and he fasted and drank no wine, and you said, 'He has a demon in him!' [34] The Son of Man came, and he ate and drank, and you said, 'Look at this man! He is a glutton and wine drinker, a friend of tax collectors and other outcasts!' [35] God's wisdom, however, is shown to be true by all who accept it." [36] A Pharisee invited Jesus to have dinner with him, and Jesus went to his house and sat down to eat. [37] In that town was a woman who lived a sinful life.

She heard that Jesus was eating in the Pharisee's house, so she brought an alabaster jar full of perfume [38] and stood behind Jesus, by his feet, crying and wetting his feet with her tears. Then she dried his feet with her hair, kissed them, and poured the perfume on them. [39] When the Pharisee saw this, he said to himself, "If this man really were a prophet, he would know who this woman is who is touching him; he would know what kind of sinful life she lives!" [40] Jesus spoke up and said to him, "Simon, I have something to tell you." "Yes, Teacher," he said, "tell me." [41] "There were two men who owed money to a moneylender," Jesus began. "One owed him five hundred silver coins, and the other owed him fifty. [42] Neither of them could pay him back, so he canceled the debts of both. Which one, then, will love him more?" [43] "I suppose," answered Simon, "that it would be the one who was forgiven more." "You are right," said Jesus. [44] Then he turned to the woman and said to Simon, "Do you see this woman? I came into your home, and you gave me no water for my feet, but she has washed my feet with her tears and dried them with her hair. [45] You did not welcome me with a kiss, but she has not stopped kissing my feet since I came. [46] You provided no olive oil for my head, but she has covered my feet with perfume. [47] I tell you, then, the great love she has shown proves that her many sins have been forgiven. But whoever has been forgiven little shows only a little love." [48] Then Jesus said to the woman, "Your sins are forgiven."

Fill in the blanks as a family before you continue:

- Jesus said, "To what can I compare the people of this _____?" "They are like children sitting in the _____ and shouting out to each other."

   Answer: (day, marketplace)

- A woman who had lived a sinful life in that town learned that Jesus was eating at the Pharisee's house, so she brought a jar of _____. As she stood behind Jesus at His feet weeping, she wet His feet with her _____ and wiped them with her hair.

   Answer: (perfume, tears)

- Jesus said, "whoever has been forgiven little shows only a _____ love."

   Answer: (little)

Family and Kid-Friendly Questions for Discussion

1. Why was Jesus amazed by the Roman officer's faith?

   Parent/Adult Tip: The officer believed Jesus could heal just by speaking a word. This teaches our kids that faith doesn't require seeing, just trusting. This can be hard because the world tells us we have to see to believe, but remind them that Jesus honors faith and trust in Him. It doesn't matter who trusts Him but how much they trust Him.

Ask: What does it mean to trust Jesus even when we can't see Him? Have you ever prayed and believed that Jesus could help you? What does amazing faith look like in your life?

2. Why do you think Jesus cared about the widow's sadness?

   Parent/Adult Tip: Jesus saw the woman's pain and acted with compassion. Teach your child that Jesus notices our sadness and wants to comfort us no matter how big or small our situation. Talk about the importance of showing kindness to others who are hurting.

   Ask: Have you ever seen someone sad and wanted to help? What can we do when someone in our family or class is hurting? How do you think Jesus helps us when we're sad?

3. Why did John the Baptist send messengers to ask whether Jesus was the Messiah?

   Parent/Adult Tip: Even strong believers have questions. Let your kids know it's okay to ask hard questions about faith. God understands and wants us to want to know more and understand. What matters is bringing those questions to Jesus, just like John did. Children can bring their questions to God through prayer or family discussions or family prayer.

   Ask: Do you ever have questions about God or faith? What do you think Jesus wants us to do when we don't understand something? How can we grow closer to God when we're unsure?

4. Why didn't some people accept Jesus, even after seeing His miracles?

Luke 7 – Jesus Helps and Heals

Parent/Adult Tip: Sometimes, people ignore the truth because it challenges them. Help your kids think about listening to Jesus, even when it's hard. Some people know that Jesus is King, but it's hard for them to follow God. It's hard to do the right thing and turn away from sin because we are comfortable, even when we know it's not the right thing to do. Share a time when following Jesus wasn't easy for you.

Ask: Why do you think some people turned away from Jesus? Is it sometimes hard to do what Jesus says? Why? What helps you listen to Him better?

5. Why did Jesus praise the sinful woman who washed His feet?

   Parent/Adult Tip: This story teaches kids that no one is too far gone for God's love. When we come to Jesus with a sorry heart, He forgives and welcomes us. Remind your children that God loves them no matter what. God wants us to turn back to Him, always.

   Ask: What does it mean to repent or say sorry to Jesus? Why did Jesus forgive the woman in the story so freely? How can we show our love for Jesus like she did?

6. Why did Jesus say those who are forgiven much, love much?

   Parent/Adult Tip: Kids can learn that being grateful for forgiveness leads to a loving heart. Encourage them to reflect on Jesus's grace and how that inspires love toward others. People who have committed the most sin are the most grateful for God's grace. I love this parable because He compares our sin with money. If you borrowed five dollars, and the lender forgave your debt, you would be grateful. But if you borrowed $10,000 and the lender said your debt was forgiven so you wouldn't have to pay that money back, how grateful would you be compared to the forgiveness of five dollars? I don't know about you, but I have sinned a lot, and I'm so thankful God loves me and forgives me every time.

Ask: What does Jesus forgive you for? How does it make you feel knowing He still loves you? How can you show love to Jesus in return? What kind of love do you have for God?

> **Closing Prayer:** *God, we thank You for being a mighty healer. Help our family have crazy faith just as the people in today's chapter of Luke did. We know that You are still healing today as You did back then, so we ask for healing in our family, and we trust You. Thank You for forgiving us each day even though we don't deserve it. Help us be more like You and be kind to others. In Jesus's name, we pray. Amen.*

Day 8

Luke 8 – Jesus's Power over Nature

Memory Verse of the Week: *"Love the Lord your God with all your heart, soul, strength, and mind. And love your neighbors as much as you love yourself"* (Luke 10:27).

Luke 8 – Jesus's Power over Nature

Say the memory verse together as a family. Then ask everyone to write the verse down a few times and put it on a sticky note in a visible location (e.g., on the bathroom mirror or as the background on their cell phones). Make sure to quiz each other throughout the week and encourage one another. You got this!

Remember to put God first and love everyone, even people you don't like.

> **Opening Prayer:** *King Jesus, help us listen carefully to Your words, just like the seeds in good soil. We want today's words to be planted and used in our daily lives, not just going in one ear and out the other. Teach our family to grow in faith and hear from You individually. In Your name, we pray. Amen.*

Luke 8:1-8

[1] Soon after this, Jesus was going through towns and villages, telling the good news about God's kingdom. His twelve apostles were with him, [2] and so were some women who had been healed of evil spirits and all sorts of diseases. One of the women was Mary Magdalene, who once had seven demons in her. [3] Joanna, Susanna, and many others had also used what they owned to help Jesus and His disciples. Joanna's husband was Chuza and one of Herod's officials. [4] When a large crowd gathered from several towns had gathered around Jesus, he told them this story: [5] "A farmer went out to scatter seed in a field. While the farmer was doing this, some of the seeds fell along the road and were stepped on or

eaten by birds. ⁶ Other seeds fell on rocky ground and started growing. But the plants did not have enough water and soon dried up. ⁷ Some other seeds fell where thornbushes grew up and choked the plants. ⁸ The rest of the seeds fell on good ground where they grew and produced a hundred times as many seeds. When Jesus has finished speaking, he said, "If you have ears to hear, pay attention."

Fill in the blanks as a family before you continue:

- Jesus traveled from town to town, spreading the _____ about God's kingdom, with His twelve apostles and some women who had been healed.

Answer: (good news)

- In the parable of the sower, Jesus described how a farmer scattered _____ , but some fell along a road, some on rocky ground, some among thornbushes, and some on good ground.

Answer: (seeds)

Luke 8:9-18

⁹ Jesus' disciples asked him what the story meant. ¹⁰ So he answered: I have explained the secrets about God's kingdom to you. But for others I use stories, so they will look, but not see, and hear, but not understand. ¹¹ This is what the story means: The seed is God's message, ¹² and the seeds that fell along the road are the people who hear that message. But the devil comes and snatches the message out of their hearts, so they will not believe and be saved. ¹³ The seeds that fell

on rocky ground are the people who gladly hear the message and accept it. But they don't have deep roots, and they believe only for a little while. As soon as life gets hard, they give up. ¹⁴ The seeds that fell among the thornbushes are those people who hear the message. But they are so eager for riches and pleasures that they never produce anything. ¹⁵ Those seeds that fell on good ground are the people who listen to the message and keep it in good and honest hearts. They last and produce a harvest.

¹⁶ "No one lights a lamp and puts it under a bowl or under a bed. A lamp is always put on a lampstand, so people will see the light. ¹⁷ There is nothing hidden that will not be found. There is no secret that will not be well known. ¹⁸ Pay attention to how you listen! Everyone who has something will be given more, but people who have nothing will lose what little they think they have.

Fill in the blanks as a family before you continue:

- Jesus explained that the seed in the story (parable) represents the _____ , and different types of ground show how people respond to it.

Answer: (God's message)

Luke 8:19-25

¹⁹ Jesus' mother and brothers came to see him, but because of the crowd they could not get near him. ²⁰ Someone told Jesus, "Your mother and brothers are standing outside and want to see you." ²¹ Jesus answered, "My mother and my

brothers are those people who hear and obey God's message." ²² One day, Jesus said to his disciples got into a boat, and he said, "Let's cross the lake." They started out, ²³ and while they were sailing across, he fell asleep. Suddenly a storm struck the lake, and the boat started sinking. They were in danger. ²⁴ So they went to Jesus and woke him up, "Master, Master! We are about to drown!" Jesuse got up and ordered the wind and the waves to stop. They obeyed, and everything was calm. ²⁵ Then Jesus asked the disciples, "Don't you have any faith?" But they were frightened and amazed. They said to each another, "Who is this? He can give orders to the wind and the waves, and they obey Him!"

Fill in the blanks as a family before you continue:

- Jesus said that His true family are those who _____ and _____ God's message.

    Answer: (hear, obey)

- The disciples woke Jesus up during the storm, saying, "Master, Master! We are about to _____ !"

    Answer: (drown)

- After Jesus calmed the storm, the disciples were amazed and asked, "Who is this? He can give orders to the _____ and the _____ , and they obey him!"

    Answer: (wind, waves)

Luke 8:26-39

²⁶ Jesus and his disciples sailed across Lake Galilee and came to shore near the town of Gerasa. ²⁷ As Jesus was getting out of the boat, he was met by man from the town. The man had demons in him. He had gone naked for a long time and no longer lived in a house, but in the graveyard. ²⁸ The man saw Jesus and screamed. He knelt down in front of him and shouted, "Jesus, Son of God Most High, what do you want with me? I beg you not to torture me!" ²⁹ He said this because Jesus had already told the evil spirit to go out of him. The man had often been attacked by the demon. And even though he had been bound with chains and leg irons and kept under guard, he smashed whatever bound him. Then the demon would force him out into lonely places. ³⁰ Jesus asked the man, "What is your name?" He answered, "My name is Lots." He said this because there were lots of demons in him. ³¹ They begged Jesus not to send them to the deep pit where they would be punished. ³² A large herd of pigs was feeding there on the hillside. So the demons begged Jesus to let them go into the pigs, and Jesus let them go. ³³ Then the demons left the man and went into the pigs. The whole herd rushed down the steep bank into the lake and drowned. ³⁴ When the men taking care of the pigs saw this, they ran to spread the news in the town and on the farms. ³⁵ The people went out to see what had happened, and when they came to Jesus, they also found the man. The demons had gone out of him, and sitting there at the feet of Jesus. He had clothes on and was in his right mind. But the people were terrified. ³⁶ Then all who had seen the man healed told about it. ³⁷ Everyone from

around Gerasa begged Jesus to leave, because they were so frightened. When Jesus got into the boat to start back, [38] the man who had been healed begged to go with Him. But Jesus sent him off and said, [39] "Go back home and tell everyone how much God has done for you." The man went all over town, telling everything that Jesus had done for him.

Fill in the blanks as a family before you continue:

- When Jesus arrived near the town of Gerasa, He met a man who was controlled by many _____ and lived in the graveyard.

Answer: (demons)

- Jesus sent the demons into a herd of _____ , which then ran into the lake and drowned.

Answer: (pigs)

- "The man then went all over town, telling everything _____ had done for him."

Answer: (Jesus)

Luke 8:40-56

[40] Everyone had been waiting for Jesus, and when he came back, a crown was there to welcome him. [41] Just then the man in charge of the synagogue came and knelt down in front of Jesus. His name was Jairus, and he begged Jesus to come to his home [42] because his twelve-year-old child was dying. She was his only daughter. While Jesus was on his

way, people were crowding all around him. ⁴³ In the crowd was a woman who had been bleeding for twelve years. She had spent everything she had on doctors, but none of them could make her well. ⁴⁴ As soon as she came up behind Jesus and barely touched his clothes, her bleeding stopped. ⁴⁵ "Who touched me?" Jesus asked. While everyone was denying it, Peter said, "Master, people are crowding all around and pushing you from every side." ⁴⁶ But Jesus answered, "Someone touched me, because I felt power going out from me." ⁴⁷ The woman knew that she could not hide, so she came trembling and knelt down in front of Jesus. She told everyone why she had touched him and that she had been healed at once. ⁴⁸ Jesus said to the woman, "You are now well because of your faith. May God give you peace!"

⁴⁹ While Jesus was still speaking, someone came from Jairus' home and said, "Your daughter had died! Why bother the teacher anymore?" ⁵⁰ When Jesus heard this, he told Jairus, "Don't worry! Have faith, and your daughter will get well." ⁵¹Jesus went into the house, but he did not let anyone else go with him except Peter, John, James, and the girl's father and mother. ⁵² Everyone was crying and weeping for the girl. But Jesus said, "The child isn't dead. She is just asleep." ⁵³ The people laughed at him because they knew she was dead. ⁵⁴ Jesus took hold of the girl's hand and said, "Child, get up!" ⁵⁵ She came back to life and got right up. Jesus told them to give her something to eat. ⁵⁶ Her parents were surprised, but Jesus ordered them not to tell anyone what had happened.

Fill in the blanks as a family before you continue:

- A man named _____ , a synagogue leader, begged Jesus to heal his dying daughter.

   Answer: (Jairus)

- A woman who had been bleeding for twelve years was healed when she touched Jesus's _____ .

   Answer: (clothes)

Family and Kid-Friendly Questions for Discussion

1. Which seed from the "parable of the seeds" do you think you are right now?

   Parent/Adult Tip: This is a great chance to talk with your kids about how our hearts respond to God's Word. Remind them that it's okay to grow step by step! Some days, our hearts might feel distracted or discouraged, but God helps us grow when we keep listening and staying close to Him. Help your child reflect without shame and focus on how they can keep growing strong roots in their faith. Are they excited to learn about God but sometimes forget (rocky soil)? Do they get distracted by TV, games, or worries (thorny soil)? Or do they try their best to follow Jesus every day and read His Word (good soil)? Let kids know that faith can grow and change! Even if they feel like one type of seed now, they can ask God to help them become "good soil." Parents/Adults, be truthful and tell which seed you feel you are.

   Ask: What kind of "ground" do you think your heart is like right now—hard path, rocky soil, thorny weeds, or good soil? What are some things that help you grow closer to God and become like a seed in good soil? Are there any "weeds" (i.e., worries, distractions, peer pressure) that try to stop your faith from growing? What could we do as a family this week to water and grow our faith?

2. How do you think the disciples felt when the storm started?

   Parent/Adult Tip: Explain that the disciples were scared because the waves were big, and they thought they might sink even though Jesus was on the boat with them. Sometimes, we feel scared too, like during a thunderstorm, when we're alone, or when something hard happens. Help kids think of a time when they felt afraid and how they reacted. I love this story because it teaches that as Jesus's followers, we will go through storms; make sure your kids know that, but thank God that we always have Jesus on the boat with us. Discuss things that we can do when the storms come. For example, I taught my kids that when they are scared, they should quote Isaiah 41:10: *"Don't be afraid. I [God] am with you."* Encourage your children to pray, read Bible verses, or talk to a trusted person when we need comfort.

   Ask: How do you think the disciples felt when the storm started, even though Jesus was on the boat? Have you ever felt scared? What are some ways to remind us that Jesus is with us during those moments?

   Challenge: This week, when you feel scared or worried, take a deep breath and say, "Jesus is with me!" or quote Isaiah 41:10. See how this helps.

3. Why do you think the man who had been controlled by demons wanted to follow Jesus after he was healed?

   Parent/Adult Tip: Talk about how the man was grateful to Jesus for setting him free. He wanted to stay with Jesus, but Jesus told him to go home and tell others what God had done for him. This shows us that sharing our faith and telling others about God's goodness is important. This is why we are here on earth: We are to spread the good news of Jesus Christ.

   Ask: Have you ever felt thankful for something and wanted to tell others about it? What has God set you free from (e.g., depression, healing, anxiety)? How can we spread the good news and share how grateful we are to God?

4. Why do you think the woman wanted to touch Jesus's clothes instead of asking Him for help? If you were the woman, what would you have done?

   Parent/Adult Tip: Explain that the woman had been sick for twelve years, and nothing had helped her get better. In her condition she was not allowed to touch anyone because they would become unclean. Twelve years is a long time to live that way. She may have been shy or scared to talk to Jesus, but she believed that just touching His clothes would heal her. This shows how strong her faith was.

   Ask: Have you ever been nervous or embarrassed to ask for help? How does this story show us that Jesus always cares? How long do you think this woman has been praying for a miracle? Did she ever give up? What are you believing in God for right now? How can you show great faith like this woman did?

5. How did Jairus show his faith when asking Jesus to heal his daughter?

Parent/Adult Tip: Use this story to show that even when life feels desperate, we can go to Jesus in faith. Jairus was probably impatient, and when he heard his child was dead, he could have lost all hope. Even when it looks like all hope is gone and nothing can be fixed, we serve a mighty God with whom all things are possible. Help your children see prayer as the first place to turn when things go wrong instead of believing what the world says.

Ask: What would you have done in Jairus's situation? Why do you think Jesus told the parents not to tell anyone that He had healed the little girl? Parent/Adults, how would you have felt during this whole situation?

Closing Prayer: *Thank You, Lord, for planting Your truth in our hearts. Help us to keep growing and to live strong and faithful lives for You. We thank You for being with us in every season, and we know that any storm that comes our way that You will be with us and get us through. We love You and thank You. In Your name, we pray. Amen.*

Day 9

Luke 9 – Jesus Feeds Thousands

Challenge: Can anyone say the memory verse without looking it up? Repeat the memory verse as a family.

Memory Verse of the Week: *"Love the Lord your God with all your heart, soul, strength, and mind. . . . Love your neighbors as much as you love yourself"* (Luke 10:27).

> **Opening Prayer:** *Heavenly Father, help us understand what it means to truly follow Jesus. Give our family courage to serve others and trust You even when it's hard. We thank You for turning our little into a lot. Help our focus be on You today as we read Your Word and let it transform our hearts. In Jesus's name, we pray. Amen.*

Luke 9: 1-9 (GNT)

¹Jesus called the twelve disciples together and gave them power and authority to drive out all demons and to cure diseases. ² Then he sent them out to preach the Kingdom of God and to heal the sick, ³ after saying to them, "Take nothing with you for the trip: no walking stick, no beggar's bag, no food, no money, not even an extra shirt. ⁴ Wherever you are welcomed, stay in the same house until you leave that

Luke 9 – Jesus Feeds Thousands

town; ⁵ wherever people don't welcome you, leave that town and shake the dust off your feet as a warning to them." ⁶ The disciples left and traveled through all the villages, preaching the Good News and healing people everywhere. ⁷ When Herod, the ruler of Galilee, heard about all the things that were happening, he was very confused, because some people were saying that John the Baptist had come back to life. ⁸ Others were saying that Elijah had appeared, and still others that one of the prophets of long ago had come back to life. ⁹ Herod said, "I had John's head cut off; but who is this man I hear these things about?" And he kept trying to see Jesus.

Fill in the blanks as a family before you continue:

- Jesus gathered His _____ and gave them power to heal and cast out demons. He sent them to _____ God's kingdom and to heal the sick.

    Answer: (disciples, preach)

- When _____ heard about the miracles and teachings of Jesus, he became confused.

    Answer: (King Herod)

Luke 9:10-17 (GNT)

¹⁰ The apostles came back and told Jesus everything they had done. He took them with him, and they went off by themselves to a town named Bethsaida. ¹¹ When the crowds heard about it, they followed him. He welcomed them, spoke to

them about the Kingdom of God, and healed those who needed it. ¹² When the sun was beginning to set, the twelve disciples came to him and said, "Send the people away so that they can go to the villages and farms around here and find food and lodging, because this is a lonely place." ¹³ But Jesus said to them, "You yourselves give them something to eat." They answered, "All we have are five loaves and two fish. Do you want us to go and buy food for this whole crowd?" ¹⁴ (There were about five thousand men there.) Jesus said to his disciples, "Make the people sit down in groups of about fifty each." ¹⁵ After the disciples had done so, ¹⁶ Jesus took the five loaves and two fish, looked up to heaven, thanked God for them, broke them, and gave them to the disciples to distribute to the people. ¹⁷ They all ate and had enough, and the disciples took up twelve baskets of what was left over.

Fill in the blanks as a family before you continue:

- The apostles only had five loaves and two fish, but Jesus took the food, looked up to heaven and gave _____ ; then He gave the food to the disciples to distribute. Everyone ate until they were full, and _____ baskets of food were left over.

Answers: (thanks, twelve)

Luke 9:18-36 (GNT)

¹⁸ One day when Jesus was praying alone, the disciples came to him. "Who do the crowds say I am?" he asked them. ¹⁹ "Some say that you are John the Baptist," they answered.

"Others say that you are Elijah, while others say that one of the prophets of long ago has come back to life." [20] "What about you?" he asked them. "Who do you say I am?" Peter answered, "You are God's Messiah." [21] Then Jesus gave them strict orders not to tell this to anyone. [22] He also told them, "The Son of Man must suffer much and be rejected by the elders, the chief priests, and the teachers of the Law. He will be put to death, but three days later he will be raised to life." [23] And he said to them all, "If you want to come with me, you must forget yourself, take up your cross every day, and follow me. [24] For if you want to save your own life, you will lose it, but if you lose your life for my sake, you will save it. [25] Will you gain anything if you win the whole world but are yourself lost or defeated? Of course not! [26] If you are ashamed of me and of my teaching, then the Son of Man will be ashamed of you when he comes in his glory and in the glory of the Father and of the holy angels. [27] I assure you that there are some here who will not die until they have seen the Kingdom of God." [28] About a week after he had said these things, Jesus took Peter, John, and James with him and went up a hill to pray. [29] While he was praying, his face changed its appearance, and his clothes became dazzling white. [30] Suddenly two men were there talking with him. They were Moses and Elijah, [31] who appeared in heavenly glory and talked with Jesus about the way in which he would soon fulfill God's purpose by dying in Jerusalem. [32] Peter and his companions were sound asleep, but they woke up and saw Jesus' glory and the two men who were standing with him. [33] As the men were leaving Jesus, Peter said to him, "Master, how good it is that we are here! We will make three tents, one for you, one for

Moses, and one for Elijah." (He did not really know what he was saying.) ³⁴ While he was still speaking, a cloud appeared and covered them with its shadow; and the disciples were afraid as the cloud came over them. ³⁵ A voice said from the cloud, "This is my Son, whom I have chosen—listen to him!" ³⁶ When the voice stopped, there was Jesus all alone. The disciples kept quiet about all this and told no one at that time anything they had seen.

Fill in the blanks as a family before you continue:

- Jesus asked His disciples, "Who do the crowds say I am?" Peter answered, "You are God's _____ ."

Answer: (Messiah)

- Jesus warned His disciples not to tell anyone that He was the Messiah. He told them that the _____ must suffer many things.

Answer: (Son of Man)

- Jesus took Peter, John, and James up a hill to _____ . Elijah and _____ met with Jesus there.

Answer: (pray, Moses)

Luke 9:37-45 (GNT)

³⁷ The next day Jesus and the three disciples went down from the hill, and a large crowd met Jesus. ³⁸ A man shouted from the crowd, "Teacher! I beg you, look at my son—my only son! ³⁹ A spirit attacks him with a sudden shout and throws

Luke 9 – Jesus Feeds Thousands

him into a fit, so that he foams at the mouth; it keeps on hurting him and will hardly let him go! [40] I begged your disciples to drive it out, but they couldn't." [41] Jesus answered, "How unbelieving and wrong you people are! How long must I stay with you? How long do I have to put up with you?" Then he said to the man, "Bring your son here." [42] As the boy was coming, the demon knocked him to the ground and threw him into a fit. Jesus gave a command to the evil spirit, healed the boy, and gave him back to his father. [43] All the people were amazed at the mighty power of God. The people were still marveling at everything Jesus was doing, when he said to his disciples, [44] "Don't forget what I am about to tell you! The Son of Man is going to be handed over to the power of human beings." [45] But the disciples did not know what this meant. It had been hidden from them so that they could not understand it, and they were afraid to ask him about the matter.

Fill in the blanks as a family before you continue:

- A man brought his son to Jesus because the boy was controlled by an _____ spirit. His disciples could _____ drive it out, but Jesus could.

  Answer: (evil, not)

- Jesus told His disciples that He would be "_____ over to the power of human beings," but they didn't understand what He meant because it was hidden from them.

  Answer: (handed)

Luke 9:46-62 (GNT)

⁴⁶ An argument broke out among the disciples as to which one of them was the greatest. ⁴⁷ Jesus knew what they were thinking, so he took a child, stood him by his side, ⁴⁸ and said to them, "Whoever welcomes this child in my name, welcomes me; and whoever welcomes me, also welcomes the one who sent me. For the one who is least among you all is the greatest." ⁴⁹ John spoke up, "Master, we saw a man driving out demons in your name, and we told him to stop, because he doesn't belong to our group." ⁵⁰ "Do not try to stop him," Jesus said to him and to the other disciples, "because whoever is not against you is for you." ⁵¹ As the time drew near when Jesus would be taken up to heaven, he made up his mind and set out on his way to Jerusalem. ⁵² He sent messengers ahead of him, who went into a village in Samaria to get everything ready for him. ⁵³ But the people there would not receive him, because it was clear that he was on his way to Jerusalem. ⁵⁴ When the disciples James and John saw this, they said, "Lord, do you want us to call fire down from heaven to destroy them?" ⁵⁵ Jesus turned and rebuked them. ⁵⁶ Then Jesus and his disciples went on to another village. ⁵⁷ As they went on their way, a man said to Jesus, "I will follow you wherever you go." ⁵⁸ Jesus said to him, "Foxes have holes, and birds have nests, but the Son of Man has no place to lie down and rest." ⁵⁹ He said to another man, "Follow me." But that man said, "Sir, first let me go back and bury my father." ⁶⁰ Jesus answered, "Let the dead bury their own dead. You go and proclaim the Kingdom of God." ⁶¹ Someone else said, "I will follow you, sir; but first let me go and say good-bye to my family." ⁶² Jesus said to him,

"Anyone who starts to plow and then keeps looking back is of no use for the Kingdom of God."

Fill in the blanks as a family before you continue:

- The disciples argued about who was the _____ . Jesus told them that the greatest among them would be like a little child, humble and willing to serve others.

Answer: (greatest)

- Jesus taught that "the one who is _____ among you all is the greatest."

Answer: (least)

Family and Kid-Friendly Questions for Discussion

1. Why did Jesus tell the disciples to take nothing with them when He sent them out?

   Parent/Adult Tip: Jesus was teaching them to trust God to provide everything they needed. As Parents/Adults, we can help kids understand that trusting God sometimes means stepping out on faith even when we don't have all the answers or supplies. This helps build faith and confidence in God's care. If he takes care of the birds, surely he will take care of us.

   Ask: Would you be willing to go and take nothing with you on a trip ? Have you ever had to trust God without knowing how something would work out? What does it mean to you to depend on God?

2. Who do you say Jesus is?

   Parent/Adult Tip: Jesus asked His disciples, "Who do you say I am?" If Jesus asked you that today, what would you say? Encourage your child to think about who Jesus is to them: Is He their friend, a helper, or a leader? Peter said Jesus was the Messiah, meaning He was sent by God to save people. I have been through dark times and sometimes felt alone. But through the good and the bad, God has never left me, so I say that Jesus is the God who never left, my comforter. Let your child express their thoughts and remind them that Jesus loves them no matter what.

   Ask: For Parents/Adults and kids: What has Jesus done for you—whether it's something big or small? Who do you say Jesus is?

3. Why do you think Jesus fed the crowd of over 5,000 people with just five loaves and two fish?

   Parent/Adult Tip: Jesus wanted to show the disciples (and us) that He can do big things with small things. Share stories of how God has taken something "small" in your life and used it in a big way.

   Ask: What's something small you have (e.g., a gift or a kind action) that God could use? How can we offer what we have to God this week? How do you think the disciples reacted when He took that small amount and fed thousands with it? How would you have reacted if you were there to witness this great miracle?

4. What do you think it means to "take up your cross each day and follow Jesus"?

   Parent/Adult Tip: Explain that "taking up your cross" means choosing to follow Jesus, even when it's hard. It might mean being kind when others are not or doing the right thing even when it's not popular. For parents/adults, this might mean quitting an addiction. For kids this might mean being kind, eating healthy (let's be real; this is hard for adults too), or not giving into peer pressure.

   Ask: When have you had to make a hard but godly choice? Have there been situations at school or a get-together when you could choose to follow Jesus even if it might not seem cool to others?

5. Why did Jesus say the greatest person is the one who serves others?

   Parent/Adult Tip: The disciples argued about who was the greatest, but Jesus said the greatest person is the one who serves (the one who is the least). Help kids understand that in God's kingdom, being great isn't about being the best at sports or having the most toys. It's about being kind and helpful, and bringing others closer to God by the way we treat them and help others.

   Ask: When we say that the greatest person is the one who serves, what does that mean? How can we serve God's kingdom? How can we serve others at home, school, or church? How can we find small ways to be "great" by loving others?

   Challenge: How can we "serve" someone this week?

6. Why did Jesus say following Him means not looking back or turning away?

Parent/Adult Tip: Jesus wants followers who are committed. This doesn't mean we'll never mess up, but it does mean choosing Him daily. The two men said they wanted to wait until something ended, but God wants your now. Tomorrow is not promised, and God wants your heart and life now. Talk about how staying focused on God can help us grow and not give up when life is hard. We all have priorities, and we can make excuses, but let's put God first and live for him now and not wait.

Ask: What things sometimes distract us from Jesus? What are some things we prioritize and don't want to let go of? How can we stay focused on following Him?

Closing Prayer: *Thank You, Father, for showing us the power of Jesus and the importance of faith. You are a provider always, and we trust and have faith that You will meet our every need. Help us carry our cross and follow You daily. In Jesus's name, we pray. Amen.*

Day 10

Luke 10 – The Good Neighbor

Challenge: Can anyone say the memory verse without looking it up? Repeat the memory verse as a family.

Memory Verse of the Week: *"Love the Lord your God with all your heart, soul, strength, and mind . . . . Love your neighbors as much as you love yourself"* (Luke 10:27).

> **Opening Prayer:** *God, as we read about loving our neighbor and listening to You, help our family do both well. Teach us to serve with love and sit with You in quiet moments daily. In Jesus's name, we pray. Amen.*

Luke 10:1-12

¹Later the Lord chose 72 other followers and sent them out two by two to every town and village where he was about to go. ² He said to them: A large crop is in the fields, but there are only a few workers. Ask the Lord in charge of the harvest to send out workers to bring it in. ³ Now go, but remember, I am sending you like lambs into a pack of wolves. ⁴ Don't take along a money bag or a traveling bag or sandals. And don't waste time greeting people on the road. ⁵ As soon as you enter a home, say, "God bless this home with peace."

⁶ If the people living there are peace-loving, your prayer for peace will bless them. But if they are not peace-loving, your prayer will return to you. ⁷ Stay with the same family, eating and drinking whatever they give you, because workers are worth what they earn. Don't move around from house to house. ⁸ If the people of a town welcome you, eat whatever they offer. ⁹ Heal their sick and say, "God's kingdom will soon be here!" ¹⁰ But if the people of a town refuse to welcome you, go out into the street and say, ¹¹ "We are shaking the dust from our feet as a warning to you. And you can be sure that God's kingdom will soon be here!" ¹² I tell you that on the day of judgment the people of Sodom will get off easier than the people of that town!

Fill in the blanks as a family before you continue:

- Jesus sent out _____ followers in pairs to every town and village He planned to visit.

    (Answer: 72)

- He told them, "If the people welcome you, eat what they give you and _____ their sick."

    (Answer: heal)

- Jesus warned "that on the day of judgment the people of _____ will get off easier than the people" any town that refused to welcome Jesus's followers.

    (Answer: Sodom)

Note: Remember that Sodom was one of the cities destroyed by God with fire and sulfur for their wicked sinful ways.

Luke 10 – The Good Neighbor

Luke 10:13-20

¹³ You people of Chorazin are in for trouble! You people of Bethsaida are also in for trouble! If the miracles that took place in your towns had happened in Tyre and Sidon, the people there would have turned to God long ago. They would have dressed in sackcloth and put ashes on their heads. ¹⁴ On the day of judgment the people of Tyre and Sidon will get off easier than you will. ¹⁵ People of Capernaum, do you think you will be honored in heaven? Well, you will go down to hell! ¹⁶ My followers, whoever listens to you is listening to me. Anyone who says "No" to you is saying "No" to me. And anyone who says "No" to me is really saying "No" to the one who sent me. ¹⁷ When the 72 followers returned, they were excited and said, "Lord, even the demons obeyed when we spoke in your name!" ¹⁸ Jesus told them: I saw Satan fall from heaven like a flash of lightning. ¹⁹ I have given you the power to trample on snakes and scorpions and to defeat the power of your enemy Satan. Nothing can harm you. ²⁰ But don't be happy because evil spirits obey you. Be happy that your names are written in heaven!

Fill in the blanks as a family before you continue:

- Jesus said that towns like Chorazin and Bethsaida would be treated worse than _____ and _____ on judgment day.

(Answer: Tyre, Sidon)

- Jesus told His followers that when people rejected them, they were really rejecting _____ ."

(Answer: Him)

- The followers were happy that even demons obeyed them, but Jesus said, "Be happy because your names are written in _____ !"

(Answer: heaven)

Luke 10:21-37

²¹ At that same time, Jesus felt the joy that comes from the Holy Spirit, and he said: My Father, Lord of heaven and earth, I am grateful that you hid all this from wise and educated people and showed it to ordinary people. Yes, Father, this is what pleased you. ²² My Father has given me everything, and he is the only one who knows the Son. The only one who really knows the Father is the Son. But the Son wants to tell others about the Father, so they can know him too. ²³ Jesus then turned to his disciples and said to them in private, "You are really blessed to see what you see! ²⁴ Many prophets and kings were eager to see what you see and to hear what you hear. But I tell you they did not see or hear."

²⁵ An expert in the Law of Moses stood up and asked Jesus a question to see what he would say. "Teacher," he asked, "what must I do to have eternal life?" ²⁶ Jesus answered, "What is written in the Scriptures? How do you understand them?" ²⁷ The man replied, "The Scriptures say, 'Love the Lord your God with all your heart, soul, strength, and mind.' They also

Luke 10 – The Good Neighbor

say, 'Love your neighbors as much as you love yourself.'" ²⁸ Jesus said, "You have given the right answer. If you do this, you will have eternal life." ²⁹ But the man wanted to show that he knew what he was talking about. So he asked Jesus, "Who are my neighbors?"

³⁰ Jesus replied: As a man was going down from Jerusalem to Jericho, robbers attacked him and grabbed everything he had. They beat him up and ran off, leaving him half dead. ³¹ A priest happened to be going down the same road. But when he saw the man, he walked by on the other side. ³² Later a temple helper came to the same place. But when he saw the man who had been beaten up, he also went by on the other side. ³³ A man from Samaria then came traveling along that road. When he saw the man, he felt sorry for him ³⁴ and went over to him. He treated his wounds with olive oil and wine and bandaged them. Then he put him on his own donkey and took him to an inn, where he took care of him. ³⁵ The next morning he gave the innkeeper two silver coins and said, "Please take care of the man. If you spend more than this on him, I will pay you when I return." ³⁶ Then Jesus asked, "Which one of these three people was a real neighbor to the man who was beaten up by robbers?" ³⁷ The expert in the Law of Moses answered, "The one who showed pity."Jesus said, "Go and do the same!"

Fill in the blanks as a family before you continue:

- Jesus thanked the Father for hiding things from the wise and showing them to _____ people.

(Answer: ordinary)

- To have eternal life you must, "_____ the Lord your God with all your heart, soul, strength, and mind." And you must "Love your _____ as much as you love yourself."

    (Answer: Love, neighbor)

Luke 10:38-42

> [38] The Lord and his disciples were traveling along and came to a village. When they got there, a woman named Martha welcomed him into her home. [39] She had a sister named Mary, who sat down in front of the Lord and was listening to what he said. [40] Martha was worried about all that had to be done. Finally, she went to Jesus and said, "Lord, doesn't it bother you that my sister has left me to do all the work by myself? Tell her to come and help me!" [41] The Lord answered, "Martha, Martha! You are worried and upset about so many things, [42] but only one thing is necessary. Mary has chosen what is best, and it will not be taken away from her."

Fill in the blanks as a family before you continue:

- A woman named _____ welcomed Jesus into her home. Her sister, _____, sat at Jesus's feet and listened to what He said.

    Answer: Martha, Mary)

- Jesus told Martha that Mary had chosen what was _____, and it would not be taken away from her.

    (Answer: best)

Luke 10 – The Good Neighbor

Family and Kid-Friendly Questions for Discussion

1. Why do you think Jesus told His followers not to take extra money, bags, or sandals?

   Parent/Adult Tip: Jesus was teaching them to trust God to provide. He wanted them to depend on Him, not on things. Teach your children that faith means trusting God, even when we don't have everything figured out or packed up. This is a good time to talk about tithing and how we are supposed to trust God with our 10 percent, given cheerfully, and to know we will be provided for.

2. Jesus says not to worry about food or clothes. God feeds the birds and clothes the lilies in wonder and splendor, and we, His children, are far more valuable than birds. So let's trust him.

   Ask: Have you ever had to trust God without knowing what would happen? What makes it hard to trust God sometimes? Parents/Adults and kids, share a time God provided something you needed.

3. Why do you think Jesus sent the 72 followers out in pairs and not just by themselves?

   Parent/Adult Tip: Jesus knew that they needed each other, and so do we. Walking with others in faith helps us grow, stay accountable, and be encouraged. Just like Proverbs 13:20 says, *"Wise friends make you wise, but you hurt yourself by going around with fools."* It's important who we choose to surround ourselves with. In a sermon, Pastor Manny Arango defined what he called the "four-fifth rule." That is, if there are four people doing trouble, you will be the fifth; if there are four people doing good, you will be the fifth. As Parents/Adults, we can guide our kids to think about the people they choose to spend time with and how those friendships affect their walk with Jesus. Parents/Adults, this is a good time to look at our friendships and the examples we are setting for our kids.

Ask: Who are some of your closest friends? Do they help you grow in your faith? How do you feel when you get to serve or work on something with a good friend? Parents/Adults, can you think of a time when a strong Christian friend helped you through something?

4. Why did the religious leaders ignore the hurt man in the parable of the Good Samaritan?

   Parent/Adult Tip: Sometimes, even people who say they follow God miss opportunities to show His love. Busyness, fear, or judgment can get in the way. Talk honestly with your children about times when you've struggled to stop and help someone in need. For example, you may have been too busy or distracted to reach out to a homeless man on the side of the road or to help a friend when they were moving or to comfort or encourage them when they were heartbroken. There are so many different situations that make us wish we could have done more. Share what you've learned from those experiences. Teaching empathy starts with showing that we're all learning and growing and that in God's eyes, nobody is better than the other.

   Ask: What keeps people from helping someone in need? Have you noticed someone who needed help? What did you do? How can our family be like the good Samaritan this week?

5. Why was Martha upset with Mary? Do you ever feel that way when someone else isn't helping? Why did Jesus say Mary chose what was better?

Parent/Adult Tip: Kids often feel frustration when things don't seem "fair." Martha was doing good work, but she missed the bigger picture—the importance of being with Jesus. This is a great opportunity to teach that both helping and resting with God are important. Parents/Adults can model this balance by sharing how they choose quiet time with God amidst daily business. Remember we need God for everything, and even though life is busy, it's important for us to put him first and take time out of every day. I love this story for busy moms and dads too. We have a million things that we could be doing, but God is telling us to slow down and spend some time with Him. Let those dishes sit there, mom, and get out that Bible.

Ask: When have you felt like you were doing all the work? How did that make you feel? How do you think Jesus would want us to respond when we feel that way? What is one way you could make space to spend time with Jesus this week? What are some things that take up most of your time each day? Parents/Adults, share how you balance chores and your spiritual life or how you could improve the balance.

Closing Prayer: *Thank You, Lord, for reminding us what really matters: You. Help us to prioritize You, God, daily even with the busyness of our daily lives. Help our home be full of love, kindness, and time with You. I pray that You would speak to us in our quiet moments with You this week. In Jesus's name, we pray. Amen.*

Day 11

Luke 11 - Teach Us to Pray

Challenge: Can anyone say the memory verse without looking it up? Repeat the memory verse as a family.

Memory Verse of the Week: "Love the Lord your God with all your heart, soul, strength, and mind.... Love your neighbors as much as you love yourself" (Luke 10:27).

> **Opening Prayer:** *God, thank You for teaching us how to pray, just like Jesus taught His disciples. Help us come to You as children come to a loving Father, trusting You with everything we need. We pray that today Your Word would fill our hearts and that our family's prayer life would be transformed. In Jesus's name, we pray. Amen.*

Luke 11:1-13 (GNT)

¹One day Jesus was praying in a certain place. When he had finished, one of his disciples said to him, "Lord, teach us to pray, just as John taught his disciples." ² Jesus said to them, "When you pray, say this: 'Father: May your holy name be honored; may your Kingdom come. ³ Give us day by day the food we need. ⁴ Forgive us our sins, for we forgive everyone who does us wrong. And do not bring us to

hard testing.'" ⁵ And Jesus said to his disciples, "Suppose one of you should go to a friend's house at midnight and say, 'Friend, let me borrow three loaves of bread. ⁶ A friend of mine who is on a trip has just come to my house, and I don't have any food for him!' ⁷ And suppose your friend should answer from inside, 'Don't bother me! The door is already locked, and my children and I are in bed. I can't get up and give you anything.' ⁸ Well, what then? I tell you that even if he will not get up and give you the bread because you are his friend, yet he will get up and give you everything you need because you are not ashamed to keep on asking. ⁹ And so I say to you: Ask, and you will receive; seek, and you will find; knock, and the door will be opened to you. ¹⁰ For those who ask will receive, and those who seek will find, and the door will be opened to anyone who knocks. ¹¹ Would any of you who are fathers give your son a snake when he asks for fish? ¹² Or would you give him a scorpion when he asks for an egg? ¹³ As bad as you are, you know how to give good things to your children. How much more, then, will the Father in heaven give the Holy Spirit to those who ask him!"

Fill in the blanks as a family before you continue:

- Jesus's disciples asked Him, "Lord, teach us to _____ ."

Answer: (pray)

- Jesus said, "Ask, and you will _____ . Seek, and you will find."

(Answer: receive)

- God gives the Holy _____ to everyone who asks Him.

(Answer: Spirit)

Luke 11:14-23 (GNT)

[14] Jesus was driving out a demon that could not talk; and when the demon went out, the man began to talk. The crowds were amazed, [15] but some of the people said, "It is Beelzebul, the chief of the demons, who gives him the power to drive them out." [16] Others wanted to trap Jesus, so they asked him to perform a miracle to show that God approved of him. [17] But Jesus knew what they were thinking, so he said to them, "Any country that divides itself into groups which fight each other will not last very long; a family divided against itself falls apart. [18] So if Satan's kingdom has groups fighting each other, how can it last? You say that I drive out demons because Beelzebul gives me the power to do so. [19] If this is how I drive them out, how do your followers drive them out? Your own followers prove that you are wrong! [20] No, it is rather by means of God's power that I drive out demons, and this proves that the Kingdom of God has already come to you. [21] "When a strong man, with all his weapons ready, guards his own house, all his belongings are safe. [22] But when a stronger man attacks him and defeats him, he carries away all the weapons the owner was depending on and divides up what he stole. [23] "Anyone who is not for me is really against me; anyone who does not help me gather is really scattering.

Fill in the blanks as a family before you continue:

- A family divided against itself _____ .

(Answer: falls apart)

- Jesus said, "Anyone who is not for _____ is against me."

(Answer: me)

Luke 11:24-32 (GNT)

²⁴ "When an evil spirit goes out of a person, it travels over dry country looking for a place to rest. If it can't find one, it says to itself, 'I will go back to my house.' ²⁵ So it goes back and finds the house clean and all fixed up. ²⁶ Then it goes out and brings seven other spirits even worse than itself, and they come and live there. So when it is all over, that person is in worse shape than at the beginning." ²⁷ When Jesus had said this, a woman spoke up from the crowd and said to him, "How happy is the woman who bore you and nursed you!" ²⁸ But Jesus answered, "Rather, how happy are those who hear the word of God and obey it!" ²⁹ As the people crowded around Jesus, he went on to say, "How evil are the people of this day! They ask for a miracle, but none will be given them except the miracle of Jonah. ³⁰ In the same way that the prophet Jonah was a sign for the people of Nineveh, so the Son of Man will be a sign for the people of this day. ³¹ On the Judgment Day the Queen of Sheba will stand up and accuse the people of today, because she traveled all the way from her country to listen to King Solomon's wise teaching; and there is something here, I tell you,

greater than Solomon. ³² On the Judgment Day the people of Nineveh will stand up and accuse you, because they turned from their sins when they heard Jonah preach; and I assure you that there is something here greater than Jonah!

Fill in the blanks as a family before you continue:

- When an evil spirit leaves a person, it goes to desert places looking for a place to _____ .

(Answer: rest)

- The Son of Man will be a sign for the people of this _____ .

(Answer: day)

Luke 11:33-54 (GNT)

³³ "No one lights a lamp and then hides it or puts it under a bowl; instead, it is put on the lampstand, so that people may see the light as they come in. ³⁴ Your eyes are like a lamp for the body. When your eyes are sound, your whole body is full of light; but when your eyes are no good, your whole body will be in darkness. ³⁵ Make certain, then, that the light in you is not darkness. ³⁶ If your whole body is full of light, with no part of it in darkness, it will be bright all over, as when a lamp shines on you with its brightness." ³⁷ When Jesus finished speaking, a Pharisee invited him to eat with him; so he went in and sat down to eat. ³⁸ The Pharisee was surprised when he noticed that Jesus had not washed before eating. ³⁹ So the Lord said to him, "Now then, you Pharisees clean the outside of your cup and plate, but inside you are

full of violence and evil. ⁴⁰ Fools! Did not God, who made the outside, also make the inside? ⁴¹ But give what is in your cups and plates to the poor, and everything will be ritually clean for you. ⁴² "How terrible for you Pharisees! You give to God one tenth of the seasoning herbs, such as mint and rue and all the other herbs, but you neglect justice and love for God. These you should practice, without neglecting the others. ⁴³ "How terrible for you Pharisees! You love the reserved seats in the synagogues and to be greeted with respect in the marketplaces. ⁴⁴ How terrible for you! You are like unmarked graves which people walk on without knowing it." ⁴⁵ One of the teachers of the Law said to him, "Teacher, when you say this, you insult us too!" ⁴⁶ Jesus answered, "How terrible also for you teachers of the Law! You put onto people's backs loads which are hard to carry, but you yourselves will not stretch out a finger to help them carry those loads. ⁴⁷ How terrible for you! You make fine tombs for the prophets—the very prophets your ancestors murdered. ⁴⁸ You yourselves admit, then, that you approve of what your ancestors did; they murdered the prophets, and you build their tombs. ⁴⁹ For this reason the Wisdom of God said, 'I will send them prophets and messengers; they will kill some of them and persecute others.' ⁵⁰ So the people of this time will be punished for the murder of all the prophets killed since the creation of the world, ⁵¹ from the murder of Abel to the murder of Zechariah, who was killed between the altar and the Holy Place. Yes, I tell you, the people of this time will be punished for them all! ⁵² "How terrible for you teachers of the Law! You have kept the key that opens the door to the house of knowledge; you yourselves will not go in, and you stop those who are trying to go in!" ⁵³ When Jesus left that place, the teachers of the Law and the Pharisees began to criticize him bitterly and ask him questions about many things, ⁵⁴ trying to lay traps for him and catch him saying something wrong.

Fill in the blanks as a family before you continue:

- Jesus said no one lights a lamp and hides it; instead, they put it on a _____ .

    Answer: (lampstand)

- Jesus told the Pharisees that they washed the outside of their cups, but they were full of greed and _____ on the inside.

    Answer: (evil)

- Jesus told the Pharisees, "You have kept the key that opens the door to the house of knowledge [about God]; you yourselves will not go in," and you keep _____ from trying to go in.

    Answer: (others)

Family and Kid-Friendly Questions for Discussion

1. Why did Jesus teach the disciples how to pray?

    Parent/Adult Tip: Jesus showed His disciples that prayer isn't about fancy words; it's about talking to God from the heart. The Lord's Prayer gives us a model; Pastor Mitchell does an awesome job breaking down the "secrets of prayer."

Review these "secrets" as a family and watch your prayer life be transformed:

- "Prayer is not an option; it is sinful to be prayerless."
- "Pray with honesty: Be honest with God with what you need, even though He already knows this."
- "Pray with an assurance that God will hear you when you pray!"[1]

Model of the Lord's Prayer (Matthew 6:9–13 NIV):

- *Our father, in heaven, hallowed be your name.* "Start with acknowledging who you are talking to. Think about who and where God is when you begin to pray. Worship God in your time of prayer."
- *Your kingdom come, your will be done.* "Then begin praying about the things God is concerned about. For example how can we spread God's word and build his kingdom, pray for spiritual leaders and for people to be saved. (This part is not about you)."
- *Give us today our daily bread.* "Ask God for your needs and do not be ashamed. You have not because you ask not."
- *And forgive us our debts as we forgive our debtors.* "Tell God your sin and deal with it as you ask for forgiveness honestly."
- *And lead us not into temptation but deliver us from the evil one.* "This is asking God for strength in our daily lives."[2]

Parent/Adult Tip: Help your children understand that prayer can happen anytime and anywhere and that it helps us stay close to God. Remember God wants a relationship with us, every day.

He doesn't just want some prayer recited over and over; He wants an actual conversation because He wants to help us and speak to us.

Ask: When do you like to talk to God? What do you usually pray about? Do you follow this model of prayer? How will this model help change your prayer life? (For me, this has transformed my tendency from praying selfish prayers to praying what God wants for me in my life—His agenda, not mine.) How has prayer helped you through hard and good times?

2. Why is it important to forgive others when we pray?

   Parent/Adult Tip: Jesus reminds us that forgiveness goes both ways; we need God's forgiveness, and we should also forgive others. Kids can struggle with holding onto hurt or being quick to react. Help them understand that forgiveness sets us free from bitterness and shows God's love. We make mistakes daily, and God forgives us. How can we accept God's forgiveness but not extend the same?

   Ask: Has someone hurt your feelings lately? Is there someone you need to forgive? Why is it hard to forgive? Share a time you had to forgive or ask for forgiveness.

3. What kind of gifts does God give His children?

   Parent/Adult Tip: Jesus compares God's generosity to a loving parent giving good gifts. Unlike people, God's gifts are always good, perfect, and given in love. Help children see that God's gift is the Holy Spirit. The Holy Spirit gives us peace, wisdom, and love; we just have to ask.

Here is a list of some spiritual gifts from Impact Nations website:[3]

- **Prophecy:** The ability to receive and proclaim a message from God.
- **Serving:** The talent to faithfully serve others and help in their needs, often behind the scenes.
- **Teaching:** The capability to teach from the Bible accurately and apply its lessons to life.
- **Encouragement:** Offering comfort, motivation, and reassurance to others.
- **Giving:** The readiness to give resources with generosity and cheerfulness.
- **Leadership:** The aptitude for leading, managing, and steering the church or its groups with diligence and dedication.
- **Mercy:** Showing deep empathy and compassion for the suffering and needy.
- **Healing:** The miraculous power to cure illness and restore health.
- **Wisdom:** The gift of making wise decisions and giving counsel according to God's will.
- **Knowledge:** The ability to understand, organize, and effectively use information for the edification of the church.
- **Faith:** Exhibiting exceptionally strong trust in God and His promises, inspiring others.

Ask: What's the best gift God has given you so far? What is one thing you'd like to ask God for today (besides stuff)? What "spiritual gift" has God given your family? If you are not sure about your spiritual gifts, this is a great time to take a couple minutes and write a prayer in your journal asking God to show you what your spiritual gifts are.

4. Why were people accusing Jesus of using evil power to cast out demons?

   Parent/Adult Tip: People didn't understand Jesus's power, so some accused Him out of fear and confusion. Help kids understand that when we follow Jesus, others may not understand our faith and try to put us down for it. We can trust that God knows the truth.

   Ask: Have you ever felt misunderstood when you were trying to do the right thing? What can you do when others question your faith? How can we, as a family, stand firm in our beliefs even when others don't get it?

5. What does Jesus mean when He says, "Anyone who is not for me is really against me"?

   Parent/Adult Tip: Jesus was calling people to choose; He wanted them to know that faith isn't something we do halfway. We do not want to be lukewarm Christians, with one foot in and one foot out. Talk with your children about fully following Jesus with our actions, not just our words.

   Discuss how they act at home, school, with friends, and at church. Is their behavior the same wherever they go? Why or why not?

Ask: What does it look like to be "with Jesus" in your everyday life? Are there moments when you feel pulled away from Him? Share a personal moment when you had to choose Jesus over something else.

6. Why did Jesus say we should be like lamps, shining brightly?

   Parent/Adult Tip: Jesus wants our lives to shine with His love so others can see Him through us. Help kids think about what it means to live as a light in their school, home, and community by being kind, honest, and full of love.

   Ask: What's one way you can be a light this week? What do you think people "see" when they look at your actions? How do you try to reflect Jesus in daily life?

7. What does this chapter teach us about prayer, light, and real faith?

   Parent/Adult Tip: Luke 11 ties prayer, truth, and action together, teaching us to talk to God, live out our faith, and shine His light. Remind your children that faith is lived daily through relationship with Jesus, kindness toward others, and a heart full of God's love.

   Ask: Which lesson from today's chapter stood out the most to you? How can we live out what we learned as a family this week? Set a family goal together (e.g., pray together each night or help someone in need).

Closing Prayer: *Heavenly Father, thank You for hearing us when we talk to You. Help us to keep asking, seeking, and knocking like Jesus told us to. I pray that we would hear your voice and be obedient to what You want us to do, Lord. Let our prayers align with Your agenda and remove any desires that are not of You from our hearts. May we remember that You give good gifts to those who love You; help us use our gifts to build Your Kingdom. In Jesus's name, we pray. Amen.*

Day 12

Luke 12 - Don't Worry

Challenge: Can anyone say the memory verse without looking it up? Repeat the memory verse as a family.

Memory Verse of the Week: *"Love the Lord your God with all your heart, soul, strength, and mind . . . . Love your neighbors as much as you love yourself"* (Luke 10:27).

Opening Prayer: *Father God, we come to You today wanting to trust You more. Jesus told us not to worry about anything but to put our trust in Him. Help us to believe that You care about the little things in our lives like You care for the birds and flowers. In Jesus's name, we pray. Amen.*

Luke 12 – Don't Worry

Luke 12:1-12

¹As thousands of people crowded around Jesus and were stepping on each other, he told his disciples: Be sure to guard against the dishonest teaching of the Pharisees! It is their way of fooling people. ² Everything that is hidden will be found out, and every secret will be known. ³ Whatever you say in the dark will be heard when it is day. Whatever you whisper in a closed room will be shouted from the housetops. ⁴ My friends, don't be afraid of people. They can kill you, but after that, there is nothing else they can do. ⁵ God is the one you must fear. Not only can he take your life, but he can throw you into hell. God is certainly the one you should fear! ⁶ Five sparrows are sold for only a few cents, but God doesn't forget a single one of them. ⁷ Even the hairs on your head are counted. So don't be afraid! You are worth much more than many sparrows. ⁸ If you tell others that you belong to me, the Son of Man will tell God's angels that you are my followers. ⁹ But if you reject me, you will be rejected in front of them. ¹⁰ If you speak against the Son of Man, you can be forgiven, but if you speak against the Holy Spirit, you cannot be forgiven. ¹¹ When you are brought to trial in the synagogues or before rulers or officials, don't worry about how you will defend yourselves or what you will say. ¹² At that time the Holy Spirit will tell you what to say.

Fill in the blanks as a family before you continue:

- Everything that is hidden will be _____ , and everything secret will be known.

Answer: (found out)

- Jesus said not to be afraid of people who can kill the body, but to fear _____ instead.

  Answer: (God)

- The Holy Spirit will help you know what to _____ when you are put on the spot.

  Answer: (say)

Luke 12:13-31

¹³ A man in a crowd said to Jesus, "Teacher, tell my brother to give me my share of what our father left us when he died." ¹⁴ Jesus answered, "Who gave me the right to settle arguments between you and your brother?" ¹⁵ Then he said to the crowd, "Don't be greedy! Owning a lot of things won't make your life safe." ¹⁶ So Jesus told them this story: A rich man's farm produced a big crop, ¹⁷ and he said to himself, "What can I do? I don't have a place large enough to store everything." ¹⁸ Later, he said, "Now I know what I'll do. I'll tear down my barns and build bigger ones, where I can store all my grain and other goods. ¹⁹ Then I'll say to myself, 'You have stored up enough good things to last for years to come. Live it up! Eat, drink, and enjoy yourself.'" ²⁰ But God said to him, "You fool! Tonight you will die. Then who will get what you have stored up?" ²¹ "This is what happens to people who store up everything for themselves, but are poor in the sight of God." ²² Jesus said to his disciples: I tell you not to worry about your life! Don't worry about having something to eat or wear. ²³ Life is more than food or clothing. ²⁴ Look at the

crows! They don't plant or harvest, and they don't have storehouses or barns. But God takes care of them. You are much more important than any birds. ²⁵ Can worry make you live longer? ²⁶ If you don't have power over small things, why worry about everything else? ²⁷ Look how the wild flowers grow! They don't work hard to make their clothes. But I tell you Solomon with all his wealth wasn't as well clothed as one of these flowers. ²⁸ God gives such beauty to everything that grows in the fields, even though it is here today and thrown into a fire tomorrow. Won't he do even more for you? You have such little faith! ²⁹ Don't keep worrying about having something to eat or drink. ³⁰ Only people who don't know God are always worrying about such things. Your Father knows what you need. ³¹ But put God's work first, and these things will be yours as well.

Fill in the blanks as a family before you continue:

- Jesus warned, "Don't be _____ . Owning a lot of stuff will not make you safe."

(Answer: greedy)

- In the story of the rich fool, the man stored up his crops but forgot about _____ .

(Answer: God)

- Jesus said, "Don't worry about having something to eat or wear.... Your Father knows what you need. But put God's _____ first."

(Answer: work)

Luke 12:32-48

[32] My little group of disciples, don't be afraid! Your Father wants to give you the kingdom. [33] Sell what you have and give the money to the poor. Make yourselves moneybags that never wear out. Make sure your treasure is safe in heaven, where thieves cannot steal it and moths cannot destroy it. [34] Your heart will always be where your treasure is. [35] Be ready and keep your lamps burning [36] just like those servants who wait up for their master to return from a wedding feast. As soon as he comes and knocks, they open the door for him. [37] Servants are fortunate if their master finds them awake and ready when he comes! I promise you he will get ready and let his servants sit down so he can serve them. [38] Those servants are really fortunate if their master finds them ready, even though he comes late at night or early in the morning. [39] You would surely not let a thief break into your home, if you knew when the thief was coming. [40] So always be ready! You don't know when the Son of Man will come. [41] Peter asked Jesus, "Did you say this just for us or for everyone?" [42] The Lord answered: Who are faithful and wise servants? Who are the ones the master will put in charge of giving the other servants their food supplies at the proper time? [43] Servants are fortunate if their master comes and finds them doing their job. [44] A servant who is always faithful will surely be put in charge of everything the master owns. [45] But suppose one of the servants thinks that the master won't return until late. Suppose that servant starts beating all the other servants and eats and drinks and gets drunk. [46] If that happens, the master will come on a day and at a time when the servant least expects him. That servant will then

be punished and thrown out with the servants who cannot be trusted. ⁴⁷ If servants are not ready or willing to do what their master wants them to do, they will be beaten hard. ⁴⁸ But servants who don't know what their master wants them to do will not be beaten so hard for doing wrong. If God has been generous with you, he will expect you to serve him well. But if he has been more than generous, he will expect you to serve him even better.

Fill in the blanks as a family before you continue:

- Jesus said, "My little group of disciples, don't be afraid! Your Father wants to give you the _____."

    Answer: (kingdom)

- Jesus said to be ready, like servants waiting for their master to return from a _____ feast.

    Answer: (wedding)

- Much is required from those who are given much, and even more is expected from those who are given _____.

    Answer: (more)

Luke 12:49-59

⁴⁹ I came to set fire to the earth, and I wish it were already on fire! ⁵⁰ I am going to be put to a hard test. And I will have to suffer a lot of pain until it is over. ⁵¹ Do you think that I came to bring peace to earth? No indeed! I came to make people choose sides. ⁵² A family of five will be divided,

with two of them against the other three. ⁵³ Fathers and sons will turn against one another, and mothers and daughters will do the same. Mothers-in-law and daughters-in-law will also turn against each other. ⁵⁴ Jesus said to all the people: As soon as you see a cloud coming up in the west, you say, "It's going to rain," and it does. ⁵⁵ When the south wind blows, you say, "It's going to get hot," and it does. ⁵⁶ Are you trying to fool someone? You can predict the weather by looking at the earth and sky, but you don't really know what's going on right now. ⁵⁷ Why don't you understand the right thing to do? ⁵⁸ When someone accuses you of something, try to settle things before you are taken to court. If you don't, you will be dragged before the judge. Then the judge will hand you over to the jailer, and you will be locked up. ⁵⁹ You won't get out until you have paid the last cent you owe.

Fill in the blanks as a family before you continue:

- Jesus said He came to bring _____ to the earth.

  Answer: (fire)

- When someone accuses you of something, try to _____ things before you are taken to court.

  Answer: (settle)

Family and Kid-Friendly Questions for Discussion

1. What does Jesus mean when He says everything secret will come out?

   Parent/Adult Tip: Help kids understand that God sees everything, not to scare them, but to encourage honesty and integrity. God knows your heart and knows your thoughts. The Bible says not to lie; lying is like sin creeping into our lives. Explain that everything has consequences, but tell kids that they can always be honest with you and that together you can handle any situation with God's help.

   Ask: Why is it important to be honest, even when no one is looking? Parents/Adults: Are you the same person at home, school, work, and church? (This question was already asked but it's worth repeating because the answer is important.)

2. Why is it important to speak up about your faith in Jesus?

   Parent/Adult Tip: Encourage your kids to be bold in sharing their love for Jesus, whether at school, with friends, or with family. Explain that we are here to spread the good news about Jesus to everyone. Jesus does not feel ashamed and hold back His love from us; He loves us openly, and we should do the same.

   Ask: When could you talk about Jesus this week with someone?

3. What does Jesus say about greed in the story of the rich fool?

   Parent/Adult Tip: Teach your kids that having "stuff" isn't bad, but loving it more than God or others is. I read a post on social media that said, "The only thing we can bring to heaven is our children." With this study, you are taking a great step by ensuring that happens.

Ask: What matters more than toys, clothes, or money? Are we going to be able to take these things with us when we go to Heaven? How can we be rich in God?

4. Why does Jesus tell us not to worry about what we will eat or wear?

   Parent/Adult Tip: Remind children that God knows what we need. Jesus mentions the flowers and crows and how He provides for them. God created us in His image; think how much more He cares for us than the rest of His creation. Why should we worry when God is on our side? Help children identify times that God has provided for your family. This is an opportunity for Parents/Adults and kids to share.

   Ask: What's something you have been worried about lately? Can we pray about it together?

   Prayer against Worry: Lord, thank You for loving us and always providing for us. Lord, I ask that You meet every need for (name), as they are worrying about (whatever their worry is). Let them know that You are with them and working it out for them right now and that You have a plan and purpose for their lives. I pray that You touch their heart right now, God, and whatever Your will is, Lord, let it be done. We trust You Jesus and give our worries to You right now. In Jesus's name. Amen.

Closing Prayer: *God, thank You for always being our provider. Teach us to seek Your kingdom first, and help us not to fear the future because You are with us. Help us be bold in our faith individually and as a family. Soften our hearts and do not let the treasures of this world affect our relationship with You; instead help us fill our heavenly treasures. Help our family rest in Your peace. In Jesus's name, we pray. Amen.*

Day 13

Luke 13 – God's Growing Kingdom

Challenge: Can anyone say the memory verse without looking it up? Repeat the memory verse as a family.

Memory Verse of the Week: *"Love the Lord your God with all your heart, soul, strength, and mind . . . . Love your neighbors as much as you love yourself"* (Luke 10:27).

Opening Prayer: *Heavenly Father, thank You for giving us second chances. You told a story about a tree needing more time to grow. Help us to grow in our faith and turn away from anything that keeps us from You. Let today's words be soaked into good ground so that they transform our hearts and minds. In Jesus's name, we pray. Amen.*

Luke 13:1-9 (GNT)

¹At that time some people were there who told Jesus about the Galileans whom Pilate had killed while they were offering sacrifices to God. ² Jesus answered them, "Because those Galileans were killed in that way, do you think it proves that they were worse sinners than all other Galileans? ³ No indeed! And I tell you that if you do not turn from your sins, you will all die as they did. ⁴ What about those eighteen people in Siloam who were killed when the tower fell on them? Do you suppose this proves that they were worse than all the other people living in Jerusalem? ⁵ No indeed! And I tell you that if you do not turn from your sins, you will all die as they did." ⁶ Then Jesus told them this parable: "There was once a man who had a fig tree growing in his vineyard. He went looking for figs on it but found none. ⁷ So he said to his gardener, 'Look, for three years I have been coming here looking for figs on this fig tree, and I haven't found any. Cut it down! Why should it go on using up the soil?' ⁸ But the gardener answered, 'Leave it alone, sir, just one more year; I will dig around it and put in some fertilizer. ⁹ Then if the tree bears figs next year, so much the better; if not, then you can have it cut down.'"

Fill in the blanks as a family before you continue:

- Jesus said that everyone must turn back to _____ , or they will be lost too.

Answer: (God)

- Jesus told a story about a man who planted a _____ tree that didn't grow fruit.

Answer: (fig)

- The gardener asked for one more _____ to care for the tree and help it grow fruit.

Answer: (year)

Luke 13:10-17 (GNT)

¹⁰ One Sabbath Jesus was teaching in a synagogue. ¹¹ A woman there had an evil spirit that had kept her sick for eighteen years; she was bent over and could not straighten up at all. ¹² When Jesus saw her, he called out to her, "Woman, you are free from your sickness!" ¹³ He placed his hands on her, and at once she straightened herself up and praised God. ¹⁴ The official of the synagogue was angry that Jesus had healed on the Sabbath, so he spoke up and said to the people, "There are six days in which we should work; so come during those days and be healed, but not on the Sabbath!" ¹⁵ The Lord answered him, "You hypocrites! Any one of you would untie your ox or your donkey from the stall and take it out to give it water on the Sabbath. ¹⁶ Now here is this descendant of Abraham whom Satan has kept in bonds for eighteen years; should she not be released on the Sabbath?" ¹⁷ His answer made his enemies ashamed of themselves, while the people rejoiced over all the wonderful things that he did.

Fill in the blanks as a family before you continue:

- Jesus healed a woman who had been crippled over for _____ years.

  Answer: (eighteen)

- The synagogue leader got upset because Jesus healed her on the _____.

  Answer: (Sabbath)

- Jesus said it was right to set her free, just like people untie their _____ or _____ on the Sabbath to give it something to drink.

  Answer: (ox, donkey)

Luke 13:18-35 (GNT)

[18] Jesus asked, "What is the Kingdom of God like? What shall I compare it with? [19] It is like this. A man takes a mustard seed and plants it in his field. The plant grows and becomes a tree, and the birds make their nests in its branches." [20] Again Jesus asked, "What shall I compare the Kingdom of God with? [21] It is like this. A woman takes some yeast and mixes it with a bushel of flour until the whole batch of dough rises." [22] Jesus went through towns and villages, teaching the people and making his way toward Jerusalem. [23] Someone asked him, "Sir, will just a few people be saved?" Jesus answered them, [24] "Do your best to go in through the narrow door; because many people will surely try to go in but will not be able. [25] The master of the house will get up and close the

door; then when you stand outside and begin to knock on the door and say, 'Open the door for us, sir!' he will answer you, 'I don't know where you come from!' [26] Then you will answer, 'We ate and drank with you; you taught in our town!' [27] But he will say again, 'I don't know where you come from. Get away from me, all you wicked people!' [28] How you will cry and gnash your teeth when you see Abraham, Isaac, and Jacob, and all the prophets in the Kingdom of God, while you are thrown out! [29] People will come from the east and the west, from the north and the south, and sit down at the feast in the Kingdom of God. [30] Then those who are now last will be first, and those who are now first will be last."

[31] At that same time some Pharisees came to Jesus and said to him, "You must get out of here and go somewhere else, because Herod wants to kill you." [32] Jesus answered them, "Go and tell that fox: 'I am driving out demons and performing cures today and tomorrow, and on the third day I shall finish my work.' [33] Yet I must be on my way today, tomorrow, and the next day; it is not right for a prophet to be killed anywhere except in Jerusalem. [34] "Jerusalem, Jerusalem! You kill the prophets, you stone the messengers God has sent you! How many times I wanted to put my arms around all your people, just as a hen gathers her chicks under her wings, but you would not let me! [35] And so your Temple will be abandoned. I assure you that you will not see me until the time comes when you say, 'God bless him who comes in the name of the Lord.'"

Fill in the blanks as a family before you continue:

- Jesus said God's kingdom is like a tiny _____ seed that grows into a big tree.

  Answer: mustard

- Jesus said to go in through the narrow _____ because not everyone will be able to do so.

  Answer: door

- Some people will be left outside, while people from all over the world will sit and feast in the _____ of God.

  Answer: kingdom

Family and Kid-Friendly Questions for Discussion

1. Why do you think Jesus told the people to turn back to God?

   Parent/Adult Tip: Talk about the importance of self-reflection and change. Share a story about a time you made a mistake and had to ask for forgiveness. Help your child understand that repentance means saying sorry and changing direction and then choosing to live God's way and not our way.

   Ask: Can you think of a time you said "sorry" and really meant it? How did it feel to be forgiven? Why is it important to turn back to God when we make mistakes?

2. What message does the parable of the unfruitful fig tree send to us?

   Parent/Adult Tip: Emphasize accountability and how spiritual growth isn't just about belief; it's about how we live. God judges us from the fruits we produce. We are the trees, and the figs represent fruits in our life. In the story, the fig tree produced no fruit, so the man told the gardener to chop it down and not let it take up space. God is saying the same to us; he wants to see the fruit of His spirit in our lives to show that we are not just taking up space. This is where spiritual growth comes in. Notice that the gardener has to tend to the tree for the fruits to grow, just like we have to tend to our spiritual tree in order for our fruits to grow.

Fruit of the Spirit: Love, joy, peace, patience, kindness, goodness, faithfulness, gentleness, and self-control.

Ask: What does your spiritual "fruit" look like right now in your life? How can we continue to grow spiritually in God's Word. How do we tend to our tree?

3. What did Jesus mean when He talked about the narrow door?

   Parent/Adult Tip: Explain that following Jesus sometimes means making hard or unpopular choices, but it's always worth it. Parents/Adults, give an example when following Jesus was uncool or unpopular and how you got through it. Also explain that not everyone can come through this "narrow" door. When we follow Jesus and have good morals, sometimes we have to leave people behind, and that is totally okay.

   Ask: Have you done something that was right, even when it was hard? How did that make you feel afterward? Have you ever had a friend, or someone you thought was your friend, who didn't always make right choices? Let's talk about those friendships and remember that we don't have to be mad at others, but we should pray for them.

4. What's the meaning behind "the last will be first"?

   Parent/Adult Tip: Talk about God's upside-down kingdom, where humility matters more than status. Talk about status at school and compare it to God's kingdom.

   Ask: Have you ever felt like you were "last" or felt that if you had more or were more popular, you would be happier? Is being popular or rich needed for God's kingdom? How can God use you as you are to better his kingdom?

5. How can your personal faith grow like a mustard seed into something strong?

   Parent/Adult Tip: Encourage setting spiritual goals and habits, journaling, reading Scripture, and serving others. The Bible says that God's kingdom is like a mustard seed that grows into a tree. Our faith needs to be like that mustard seed and grow into something big and keep growing.

   Ask: What's one new habit or change you'd like to try this week to grow closer to God? Let's make a goal to grow our faith and hold each other accountable.

> **Closing Prayer:** *Father, thank You for being patient with us. Help us to learn from Your Word and bear good fruit in our lives. Give our family wisdom to know when to let go of seasons and people so that we can go through your narrow door, Lord. May our family grow stronger in faith and love each day. In Jesus's name, we pray. Amen.*

Day 14

Luke 14 – A Special Invitation

Challenge: Can anyone say the memory verse without looking it up? Repeat the memory verse as a family.

Memory Verse of the Week: *"Love the Lord your God with all your heart, soul, strength, and mind . . . . Love your neighbors as much as you love yourself"* (Luke 10:27).

> **Opening Prayer:** *God, thank You for inviting us to follow You. Jesus showed us that being humble and caring for others is important to You, so we pray that You would touch our hearts and remove any bad and help us be more like Jesus. Help us treat others kindly and put them before ourselves. In Jesus's name, we pray. Amen.*

Luke 14:1-14

¹ One Sabbath, Jesus was having dinner in the home of an important Pharisee, and everyone was carefully watching Jesus. ² All of a sudden a man with swollen legs stood up in front of him. ³ Jesus turned and asked the Pharisees and the teachers of the Law of Moses, "Is it right to heal on the Sabbath?" ⁴ But they did not say a word. Jesus took hold of the man. Then he healed him and sent him away. ⁵ Afterwards,

Jesus asked the people, "If your son or ox falls into a well, wouldn't you pull him out at once, even on the Sabbath?" [6] There was nothing they could say. [7] Jesus saw how the guests had tried to take the best seats. So he told them: [8] When you are invited to a wedding feast, don't sit in the best place. Someone more important may have been invited. [9] Then the one who invited you will come and say, "Give your place to this other guest!" You will be embarrassed and will have to sit in the worst place. [10] When you are invited to be a guest, go and sit in the worst place. Then the one who invited you may come and say, "My friend, take a better seat!" You will then be honored in front of all the other guests. [11] If you put yourself above others, you will be put down. But if you humble yourself, you will be honored. [12] Then Jesus said to the man who had invited him: When you give a dinner or a banquet, don't invite your friends and family and relatives and rich neighbors. If you do, they will invite you in return, and you will be paid back. [13] When you give a feast, invite the poor, the paralyzed, the lame, and the blind. [14] They cannot pay you back. But God will bless you and reward you when his people rise from death.

Fill in the blanks as a family before you continue:

- Jesus noticed how the guests at the Pharisee's house picked the best places to sit, so He told a story to teach about choosing to be _____ instead of putting yourself first.

Answer: (humble)

- Instead of inviting people who can repay you, Jesus said to invite the poor, crippled, lame, and blind—people who _____ pay you back.

    Answer: (cannot)

Luke 14:15-24

¹⁵ After Jesus had finished speaking, one of the guests said, "The greatest blessing of all is to be at the banquet in God's kingdom!" ¹⁶ Jesus told him: A man once gave a great banquet and invited a lot of guests. ¹⁷ When the banquet was ready, he sent a servant to tell the guests, "Everything is ready! Please come." ¹⁸ One guest after another started making excuses. The first one said, "I bought some land, and I've got to look it over. Please excuse me." ¹⁹ Another guest said, "I bought five teams of oxen, and I need to try them out. Please excuse me." ²⁰ Still another guest said, "I've just now married, and I can't be there." ²¹ The servant told his master what happened, and the master became so angry he said, "Go as fast as you can to every street and alley in town! Bring in everyone who is poor or paralyzed or blind or lame." ²² When the servant returned, he said, "Master, I've done what you told me, and there is still plenty of room for more people." ²³ His master then told him, "Go out along the back roads and make people come in, so my house will be full. ²⁴ Not one of the guests I first invited will get even a bite of my food!"

Fill in the blanks as a family before you continue:

- Jesus told a story about a man who prepared a big dinner and invited many people, but they all made _____ and didn't come.

Answer: (excuses)

- Jesus ended the story by saying that not one of the guests the man first invited would get a _____ of his food.

Answer: (bite)

Luke 14:25-35

25 Large crowds were walking along with Jesus, when he turned and said: 26 You cannot be my disciple, unless you love me more than you love your father and mother, your wife and children, and your brothers and sisters. You cannot follow me unless you love me more than you love your own life. 27 You cannot be my disciple unless you carry your own cross and follow me. 28 Suppose one of you wants to build a tower. What is the first thing you will do? Won't you sit down and figure out how much it will cost and if you have enough money to pay for it? 29 Otherwise, you will start building the tower, but not be able to finish. Then everyone who sees what is happening will laugh at you. 30 They will say, "You started building, but could not finish the job." 31 What will a king do if he has only 10,000 soldiers to defend himself against a king who is about to attack him with 20,000 soldiers? Before he goes out to battle, won't he first sit down and decide if he can win? 32 If he thinks he won't be able to

Luke 14 – A Special Invitation

defend himself, he will send messengers and ask for peace while the other king is still a long way off. ³³ So then, you cannot be my disciple unless you give away everything you own. ³⁴ Salt is good, but if it no longer tastes like salt, how can it be made to taste salty again? ³⁵ It is no longer good for the soil or even for the manure pile. People simply throw it out. If you have ears, pay attention!

Fill in the blanks as a family before you continue:

- Jesus said that if people want to follow Him, they must love Him more than they love their family or even their own _____ .

Answer: (life)

- Jesus gave an example of someone building a tower, reminding us to first think about what it will _____ to follow Him.

Answer: (cost)

- Jesus said, "Salt is good, but if it no longer tastes like salt, how can it be made to _____ salty again?"

Answer: (taste)

Family and Kid-Friendly Questions for Discussion

1. Why do you think Jesus healed the sick man even though it was the Sabbath (a day of rest)?

   Parent/Adult Tip: Emphasize that Jesus shows us that people are more important than rules. For young kids, talk about kindness. For older kids or teens, talk about when doing good might be misunderstood. Help your child see Jesus as someone who deeply cares for others and wants us to do the same, even when it's not easy or expected.

Ask: Have you ever done something good when others thought you shouldn't? How do we decide when to do what's right, even if it's not popular?

2. Jesus said it's better to sit in the lowest place at a party and be invited up. Why does that matter?

    Parent/Adult Tip: Talk about humility and not thinking we're better than others. For older kids, explain that true confidence is quiet and respectful. Remind them that Jesus sees our hearts, not just where we sit. He honors those who put others first.

    Ask: What does it mean to be humble? How does it feel when someone lifts you up instead of you pushing your way to the front? Can we think of a way to let someone else "go first" this week?

3. Why does Jesus say we should invite people who can't repay us?

    Parent/Adult Tip: Teach that love isn't a transaction; God gives freely, and we should too. Use this to spark ideas for serving others, expecting no reward. This is a great chance to model generosity and selfless giving as a family; you may want to plan a small act of kindness. Talk about donating clothes or toys to others who don't have as much as we have, or consider making care packages.

Ask: How does it feel to do something nice without expecting anything back? Can we think of someone we could bless as a family this week? Why do you think God wants us to love people who are often forgotten?

4. What does Jesus mean when He says to count the cost before following Him?

   Parent/Adult Tip: Explain that being a Christian isn't always easy; it means choosing Jesus when it's hard. Share your own experience honestly. Let kids know that Jesus always gives more than we lose, and He's worth every sacrifice.

   Ask: What might it cost us to follow Jesus at school or with friends? What do you think Jesus is asking you to give Him? Is there a part of your life you find hard to give to Jesus?

5. Why do you think salt is important in the story? What does it mean for us to "lose our flavor"?

   Parent/Adult Tip: Use examples of food: Salt adds flavor and preserves. In the same way, our lives should point others to Jesus. Challenge older kids to live boldly for Jesus, and remind younger ones that even little acts of kindness make a big difference.

   Ask: What makes someone a good example of Jesus? Have you ever seen someone act "flavorless" in their faith, just going through the motions? This could be someone who just goes to church every Sunday but never reads the Word and treats others badly. On the outside they may look like a Christian, but on the inside, they don't. Also make sure children know it's okay if that is how they feel right now. Or maybe that describes you right now. Let's use this time to do better and grow in Christ. What does it look like for us to be flavorful in our faith?

> **Closing Prayer:** *Lord, help us not to make excuses but to always say yes to Your invitation. May our family be known for our love, humility, and willingness to serve others just as You were known for acts of service. Give us the strength to do and say the right thing in tough moments. Help us be humble and remove any pride from our heart. In Your name, we pray. Amen.*

Day 15

Luke 15 – The Lost and Found

Memory Verse of the Week: *"In the same way, God's angels are happy when even one sinner turns to him"* (Luke 15:10).

Let's be the one that turns back to him **always**. Say the memory verse together as a family. Then ask everyone to write the verse down a few times and put it on a sticky note in a visible location (e.g., on the bathroom mirror or as the background on their cell phones). Make sure to quiz each other throughout the week and encourage one another. You got this!

> **Opening Prayer:** *Heavenly Father, thank You for loving us so much that You come looking for us when we're lost. We see how joyful You are when even one person comes back to You. Help us understand that kind of love. Help us remember through every mistake that Your love for us is so big that You always want us to come back. In Jesus's name, we pray. Amen.*

Luke 15:1-10 (GNT)

¹ One day when many tax collectors and other outcasts came to listen to Jesus, ² the Pharisees and the teachers of the Law started grumbling, "This man welcomes outcasts and even eats with them!" ³ So Jesus told them this parable: ⁴ "Suppose one of you has a hundred sheep and loses one of them—what do you do? You leave the other ninety-nine sheep in the pasture and go looking for the one that got lost until you find it. ⁵ When you find it, you are so happy that you put it on your shoulders ⁶ and carry it back home. Then you call your friends and neighbors together and say to them, 'I am so happy I found my lost sheep. Let us celebrate!' ⁷ In the same way, I tell you, there will be more joy in heaven over one sinner who repents than over ninety-nine respectable people who do not need to repent. ⁸ "Or suppose a woman who has ten silver coins loses one of them—what does she do? She lights a lamp, sweeps her house, and looks carefully everywhere until she finds it. ⁹ When she finds it, she calls her friends and neighbors together, and says to them, 'I am so happy I found the coin I lost. Let us celebrate!' ¹⁰ In the same

way, I tell you, the angels of God rejoice over one sinner who repents."

Fill in the blanks as a family before you continue:

- Jesus told a story about a person who had _____ sheep and lost one.

Answer: (100)

- The shepherd was so _____ when he found the lost sheep that he carried it home.

Answer: (happy)

Luke 15:11-32 (GNT)

[11] Jesus went on to say, "There was once a man who had two sons. [12] The younger one said to him, 'Father, give me my share of the property now.' So the man divided his property between his two sons. [13] After a few days the younger son sold his part of the property and left home with the money. He went to a country far away, where he wasted his money in reckless living. [14] He spent everything he had. Then a severe famine spread over that country, and he was left without a thing. [15] So he went to work for one of the citizens of that country, who sent him out to his farm to take care of the pigs. [16] He wished he could fill himself with the bean pods the pigs ate, but no one gave him anything to eat. [17] At last he came to his senses and said, 'All my father's hired workers have more than they can eat, and here I am about to starve! [18] I will get up and go to my father and say,

"Father, I have sinned against God and against you. ¹⁹ I am no longer fit to be called your son; treat me as one of your hired workers.'" ²⁰ So he got up and started back to his father. "He was still a long way from home when his father saw him; his heart was filled with pity, and he ran, threw his arms around his son, and kissed him. ²¹ 'Father,' the son said, 'I have sinned against God and against you. I am no longer fit to be called your son.' ²² But the father called to his servants. 'Hurry!' he said. 'Bring the best robe and put it on him. Put a ring on his finger and shoes on his feet. ²³ Then go and get the prize calf and kill it, and let us celebrate with a feast! ²⁴ For this son of mine was dead, but now he is alive; he was lost, but now he has been found.' And so the feasting began.²⁵ "In the meantime the older son was out in the field. On his way back, when he came close to the house, he heard the music and dancing. ²⁶ So he called one of the servants and asked him, 'What's going on?' ²⁷ 'Your brother has come back home,' the servant answered, 'and your father has killed the prize calf, because he got him back safe and sound.' ²⁸ The older brother was so angry that he would not go into the house; so his father came out and begged him to come in. ²⁹ But he spoke back to his father, 'Look, all these years I have worked for you like a slave, and I have never disobeyed your orders. What have you given me? Not even a goat for me to have a feast with my friends! ³⁰ But this son of yours wasted all your property on prostitutes, and when he comes back home, you kill the prize calf for him!' ³¹ 'My son,' the father answered, 'you are always here with me, and everything I have is yours. ³² But we had to celebrate and be happy, because your brother was dead, but now he is alive; he was lost, but now he has been found.'"

Fill in the blanks as a family before you continue:

- A man had two sons, and the younger one asked for his part of the family _____ .

    Answer: (property)

- The younger son wasted all his money on wild living and ended up feeding _____ to survive.

    Answer: (pigs)

- The older brother was upset, but the father said, "We had to celebrate and be happy, because your brother was dead, but now he is alive; he was lost, but now he has been _____ ."

    Answer: found

Family and Kid-Friendly Questions for Discussion

1. Why do you think Jesus talked about lost things being found?

    Parent/Adult Tip: Jesus tells three stories to show that God searches for us no matter what. Even when we feel far away or have done something wrong, He wants us back and celebrates us. This helps kids and teens understand how deeply God cares about each person. Let your kids know that you feel the same way; we sometimes make mistakes and get lost, but all we want for our children is to learn from mistakes and find their way back.

Ask: What does the one lost sheep represent? What's something valuable you've lost and found again? How did you feel? Do you think God ever gives up on people? What does it say about God that He notices even one lost sheep?

2. In the story of the lost son, why did the father run to him and throw a party?

   Parent/Adult Tip: Talk about grace and forgiveness and the love God has for us and the love you have for your kids. Help your kids see that God doesn't hold grudges and neither should we. He rejoices when we return even after we've messed up. And guess what . . . we are going to mess up again.

   Ask: How would you feel if you were the son coming home? What do you think was going through his head? When you have gotten in trouble and had to go back to your parents for something how did you feel? What do you think the party meant? Can you think of a time you were forgiven?

3. How would you feel if you were the older brother in the story?

   Parent/Adult Tip: Use this story to talk about fairness versus grace. It seems natural to want rewards for good behavior, but Jesus teaches us that celebrating someone else's return doesn't take away our worth. This story also helps us see that wanting rewards for our good behavior is just works-based faithfulness. Instead, we should do good things out of the goodness of our hearts expecting nothing in return.

   Ask: Have you ever felt like someone else got something you deserved? Why do you think the father told the older son,

"Everything I have is yours"? Is it hard to be happy when someone else is being celebrated? Is life always fair? How can we react when it is not?

4. Why is the brother jealous of the younger brother?

   Parent/Adult Tip: Pastor Manny Arango breaks down this parable beautifully in his Arma course on the Gospel of Luke. (Side note: if you want to know more about the Bible and need help understanding it, Pastor Arango's Arma courses are amazing.) He says the focus of this parable is the son who stayed (wait . . . what?). I thought that the older son was the great one—the one who was close to the father (the insider). But Pastor Arango points out that the older brother got his share just like his younger brother. So they both had to agree to get their part.[4]

5. Explain that even though the older brother lived close to his dad, they were not close; they did not share the same heart. Wow! How many Christians do we know who are at church every Sunday but have hateful hearts? Jesus was comparing the older son to the Pharisees. They knew the Word and were "close" but did not have any love in their hearts for the broken.

   Ask: Why do you think the older brother agreed to let his brother get his part and go? What does it mean to "live close to God but not know God"? On the outside the older brother looks like he is doing all the right things, but he is not happy that his brother has returned. God's heart breaks over lost people, so why doesn't his?

Closing Prayer: *Father God, thank You for never giving up on us. Help us to be like the father in the story, always ready to forgive and love. Never let us forget that we were lost at one time, but You took the time to find us and remind us how much You love us. Let our family reflect that same kind of love and grace to others. In Jesus's name, we pray. Amen.*

Day 16

Luke 16 – Being Faithful

Challenge: Can anyone say the memory verse without looking it up? Repeat the memory verse as a family.

Memory Verse of the Week: *"In the same way, God's angels are happy when even one sinner turns to him"* (Luke 15:10).

Opening Prayer: *King Jesus, teach us to care more about what matters to You than about things that won't last. Let our identity be in what You say we are and not in what this world says. You reminded us that true riches come from faith and kindness. Help us to be faithful and generous toward others with what we have. In Jesus's name, we pray. Amen.*

Luke 16:1-18

¹ Jesus said to his disciples: A rich man once had a manager to take care of his business. But he was told that his manager was wasting money. ² So the rich man called him in and said, "What is this I hear about you? Tell me what you have done! You are no longer going to work for me."**3** The manager said to himself, "What shall I do now that my master is going to fire me? I can't dig ditches, and I'm ashamed to beg. ⁴ I know what I'll do, so that people will welcome me into their homes after I've lost my job." ⁵ Then one by one he called in the people who were in debt to his master. He asked the first one, "How much do you owe my master?" ⁶ "A hundred barrels of olive oil," the man answered. So the manager said, "Take your bill and sit down and quickly write '50.'" ⁷ The manager asked someone else who was in debt to his master, "How much do you owe?" "A thousand sacks of wheat," the man replied. The manager said, "Take your bill and write '800.'" ⁸ The master praised his dishonest manager for looking out for himself so well. That's how it is! The people of this world look out for themselves better than the people who belong to the light. ⁹ My disciples, I tell you to use wicked wealth to make friends for yourselves. Then when it is gone, you will be welcomed into an eternal home. ¹⁰ Anyone who can be trusted in little matters can also be trusted in important matters. But anyone who is dishonest in little matters will be dishonest in important matters. ¹¹ If you cannot be trusted with this wicked wealth, who will trust you with true wealth? ¹² And if you cannot be trusted with what belongs to someone else, who will give you something that will be

your own? ¹³ You cannot be the slave of two masters. You will like one more than the other or be more loyal to one than to the other. You cannot serve God and money. ¹⁴ The Pharisees really loved money. So when they heard what Jesus said, they made fun of him. ¹⁵ But Jesus told them: You are always making yourselves look good, but God sees what is in your heart. The things that most people think are important are worthless as far as God is concerned. ¹⁶ Until the time of John the Baptist, people had to obey the Law of Moses and the Books of the Prophets. But since God's kingdom has been preached, everyone is trying hard to get in. ¹⁷ Heaven and earth will disappear before the smallest letter of the Law does. ¹⁸ It is a terrible sin for a man to divorce his wife and marry another woman. It is also a terrible sin for a man to marry a divorced woman.

Fill in the blanks as a family before you continue:

- Anyone who can be trusted in _____ matters can also be trusted in important matters.

Answer: (little)

- You cannot serve both _____ and _____ .

Answer: (God, money)

- God sees what is in your _____ .

Answer: (heart)

Luke 16:19-31

There was once a rich man who wore expensive clothes and every day ate the best food. [20] But a poor beggar named Lazarus was brought to the gate of the rich man's house. [21] He was happy just to eat the scraps that fell from the rich man's table. His body was covered with sores, and dogs kept coming up to lick them. [22] The poor man died, and angels took him to the place of honor next to Abraham. The rich man also died and was buried. [23] He went to hell and was suffering terribly. When he looked up and saw Abraham far off and Lazarus at his side, [24] he said to Abraham, "Have pity on me! Send Lazarus to dip his finger in water and touch my tongue. I'm suffering terribly in this fire." [25] Abraham answered, "My friend, remember that while you lived, you had everything good, and Lazarus had everything bad. Now he is happy, and you are in pain. [26] And besides, there is a deep ditch between us, and no one from either side can cross over." [27] But the rich man said, "Abraham, then please send Lazarus to my father's home. [28] Let him warn my five brothers, so they won't come to this horrible place." [29] Abraham answered, "Your brothers can read what Moses and the prophets wrote. They should pay attention to that." [30] Then the rich man said, "No, that's not enough! If only someone from the dead would go to them, they would listen and turn to God." [31] So Abraham said, "If they won't pay attention to Moses and the prophets, they won't listen even to someone who comes back from the dead."

Fill in the blanks as a family before you continue:

- A rich man lived in luxury, but a poor man named _____ lay at his gate.

  Answer: (Lazarus)

- Abraham said, "My friend, remember that while you lived, you had everything good, and Lazarus had everything bad. Now he is happy, and you are in _____ ."

  Answer: (pain)

- Abraham responded to the rich man's request this way: "If they won't pay attention to Moses and the prophets, they won't listen even to someone who comes back from the _____ ."

  Answer: dead

Family and Kid-Friendly Questions for Discussion

1. What does it mean to be responsible with what God gives us?

   Parent/Adult Tip: Use real-life examples such as chores, toys, time, school, or money to help kids (and parents) understand that everything we have is a gift from God.

   Ask: How do you take care of your things or share with others? Can God trust you with more? How do you know He can trust you with more?

2. Why do you think Jesus said we can't serve both God and money?

   Parent/Adult Tip: Help kids and teens think about how money and stuff can distract us from what matters most. Anything that is keeping you away from God is a distraction. Sometimes, we put things before God without even realizing it. Take time as a family and write down some priorities in each person's life and share. Talk about ways we can incorporate God into those priorities and make God number one.

Ask: What are some things people (we) "chase after"? How can we show that God is first in our life?

3. What lesson can we learn from the rich man and Lazarus in this passage?

   Parent/Adult Tip: Help older kids and teens think about choices that have lasting consequences. Talk about kindness and noticing people who are hurting, lonely, or in need and how we can be generous to them. Make it clear that being generous is not all about money; there are other ways to be there for others. The rich man did the right thing, right? He gave his leftovers and scraps to Lazarus, but that was not enough. (Whew. If this parable is not convicting, I don't know what to tell you.) We give what we have left over to others, right? We are generous here and there, but God is saying that is not enough.

   Ask: Why is it important to choose God now, not later? How do we choose God? What does this story tell us about Heaven and hell? What could the rich man have done while he was alive to ensure he was going to Heaven? How can we also encourage others to choose God?

4. If you were Lazarus, how would you feel about being ignored every day?

Parent/Adult Tip: Build empathy (understanding how others feel) and compassion. This helps children think about how others feel. Consider asking whether they have ever felt this way. This is a great time to talk to kids and really have them open up about what goes on in their everyday lives.

Ask: How can we treat people like Lazarus better? Who can we include or help this week? This could be family, strangers, or people at school. Think of ways to show God's love that don't cost money.

5. Why do you think God wants us to be generous?

   Parent/Adult Tip: Explain how generosity reflects God's character and builds love. Remember the command to love God and love others means everyone. I heard a pastor say that "even people you don't like are going to go to Heaven with you," so let's work on loving everyone now.

   Ask: How does it feel when someone shares with you or gives you a compliment or includes you in things? What can you give, share, or do this week?

Closing Prayer: *Lord, thank You for trusting us with what we've been given. Help our family use our time, money, and hearts for You. I rebuke anything that tries to take Your place. Help us to prioritize You in everything. Holy Spirit, tell us who to help and how. I pray You never let our heads get so big that we think we can do things without You. In Your name, we pray. Amen.*

Day 17

Luke 17 - The Grateful One

Challenge: Can anyone say the memory verse without looking it up? Repeat the memory verse as a family.

Memory Verse of the Week: *"In the same way, God's angels are happy when even one sinner turns to him"* (Luke 15:10).

> **Opening Prayer:** *King Jesus, You taught us to forgive over and over again and to have faith even as small as a mustard seed. Help our family to forgive quickly and believe boldly. Help us always be grateful every day for all You have done for us. We know that without You, Lord, we cannot do life. We love You and ask that our focus be on You today. In Your name, we pray. Amen.*

Luke 17:1-10 (GNT)

¹ Jesus said to his disciples, "Things that make people fall into sin are bound to happen, but how terrible for the one who makes them happen! ² It would be better for him if a large millstone were tied around his neck and he were thrown into the sea than for him to cause one of these little ones to sin. ³ So watch what you do! "If your brother sins, rebuke him, and if he repents, forgive him. ⁴ If he sins against you seven times

in one day, and each time he comes to you saying, 'I repent,' you must forgive him." ⁵ The apostles said to the Lord, "Make our faith greater." ⁶ The Lord answered, "If you had faith as big as a mustard seed, you could say to this mulberry tree, 'Pull yourself up by the roots and plant yourself in the sea!' and it would obey you. ⁷ "Suppose one of you has a servant who is plowing or looking after the sheep. When he comes in from the field, do you tell him to hurry along and eat his meal? ⁸ Of course not! Instead, you say to him, 'Get my supper ready, then put on your apron and wait on me while I eat and drink; after that you may have your meal.' ⁹ The servant does not deserve thanks for obeying orders, does he? ¹⁰ It is the same with you; when you have done all you have been told to do, say, 'We are ordinary servants; we have only done our duty.'"

Fill in the blanks as a family before you continue:

- We should be careful not to cause others to _____, especially those who are young in faith.

Answer: (sin)

- If someone does something wrong to us and says they're sorry, we should _____ them, even if it happens many times.

Answer: (forgive)

- Servants don't deserve special thanks for doing what they are _____ to do.

Answer: (supposed)

Luke 17:11-19 (GNT)

¹¹ As Jesus made his way to Jerusalem, he went along the border between Samaria and Galilee. ¹² He was going into a village when he was met by ten men suffering from a dreaded skin disease. They stood at a distance ¹³ and shouted, "Jesus! Master! Have pity on us!" ¹⁴ Jesus saw them and said to them, "Go and let the priests examine you." On the way they were made clean. ¹⁵ When one of them saw that he was healed, he came back, praising God in a loud voice. ¹⁶ He threw himself to the ground at Jesus' feet and thanked him. The man was a Samaritan. ¹⁷ Jesus spoke up, "There were ten who were healed; where are the other nine? ¹⁸ Why is this foreigner the only one who came back to give thanks to God?" ¹⁹ And Jesus said to him, "Get up and go; your faith has made you well."

Fill in the blanks as a family before you continue:

- Ten men with a skin disease asked Jesus to have _____ on them.

Answer: (pity)

- Jesus told the thankful man, "Your _____ has made you well."

Answer: (faith)

Luke 17:20-37 (GNT)

²⁰ Some Pharisees asked Jesus when the Kingdom of God would come. His answer was, "The Kingdom of God does

not come in such a way as to be seen. ²¹ No one will say, 'Look, here it is!' or, 'There it is!'; because the Kingdom of God is within you." ²² Then he said to the disciples, "The time will come when you will wish you could see one of the days of the Son of Man, but you will not see it. ²³ There will be those who will say to you, 'Look, over there!' or, 'Look, over here!' But don't go out looking for it. ²⁴ As the lightning flashes across the sky and lights it up from one side to the other, so will the Son of Man be in his day. ²⁵ But first he must suffer much and be rejected by the people of this day. ²⁶ As it was in the time of Noah so shall it be in the days of the Son of Man. ²⁷ Everybody kept on eating and drinking, and men and women married, up to the very day Noah went into the boat and the flood came and killed them all. ²⁸ It will be as it was in the time of Lot. Everybody kept on eating and drinking, buying and selling, planting and building. ²⁹ On the day Lot left Sodom, fire and sulfur rained down from heaven and killed them all. ³⁰ That is how it will be on the day the Son of Man is revealed. ³¹ "On that day someone who is on the roof of a house must not go down into the house to get any belongings; in the same way anyone who is out in the field must not go back to the house. ³² Remember Lot's wife! ³³ Those who try to save their own life will lose it; those who lose their life will save it. ³⁴ On that night, I tell you, there will be two people sleeping in the same bed: one will be taken away, the other will be left behind. ³⁵ Two women will be grinding meal together: one will be taken away, the other will be left behind." ³⁶⁻³⁷ The disciples asked him, "Where, Lord?" Jesus answered, "Wherever there is a dead body, the vultures will gather."

Fill in the blanks as a family before you continue:

- Jesus said the Kingdom of God is not something you can see coming; it's _____ with you.

    Answer: (within)

- People who try to save their lives will lose them, and those who lose their lives will _____ them.

    Answer: (save)

Family and Kid-Friendly Questions for Discussion

1. What does it mean to forgive someone again and again?

    Parent/Adult Tip: Jesus tells us in Luke 17:3–4 to forgive others even if they hurt us many times. Explain that forgiveness doesn't always mean trusting someone the same way, but it means not holding hate in our hearts. Remind them that we have made plenty of mistakes in our lives, and God has forgiven us time and time again even though we are undeserving. So if we want to accept God's forgiveness, we need to do the same for others.

    Ask: Has anyone ever made you upset more than once? What helped you forgive them? Is there anyone in your life who is hard to forgive, or is there someone you haven't forgiven? Do we have to remain close to someone who continues to hurt us? How can we forgive and remove ourselves?

2. What does it mean to cause someone else to sin, and why does Jesus say that is such a big deal?

Parent/Adult Tip: Jesus talks about how serious it is to lead others into doing wrong. Especially for kids and teens, our words and actions can influence others. Parents, we are the ultimate influencers in our kids' lives; our actions can lead them into sin or steer them away. Help your children understand that when we tease, lie, pressure someone to do something wrong, or set a bad example, we may be causing someone else to sin. This is something Jesus wants us to be very careful about. Encourage kids of all ages to think about how they treat others, especially siblings, friends, or classmates. Are they being a good or bad influence? Let your kids know that Jesus wants us to help each other do what's right, not what's wrong. Let's be good examples of followers of Christ.

Ask: Can you think of a time someone copied something you did, good or bad?"

Have you ever laughed when someone else was being mean? How could that encourage more wrong behavior? Do you think what we post or say online can cause others to sin or act badly? Why or why not? What are some ways we can be a godly influence among friends, even when it's hard? Parents/adults, how can our actions cause our kids to sin or not to sin?

3. Of the ten lepers who were healed, what made one man come back to thank Jesus after being healed?

    Parent/Adult Tip: One man who had been healed showed a heart of thankfulness. Encourage your children to recognize blessings and give thanks often.

Ask: What is something you are thankful for today? How do you show gratitude to God in your everyday life?

4. Why do you think the other nine people didn't come back?

   Parent/Adult Tip: Kids may assume that being healed is enough. Help them see that Jesus desires a relationship with us, not just requests. Yes, he is a good God and will answer our prayers, but we must continue to praise Him, spend time with Him in good and bad times, and be thankful regardless of the season. I'm glad we have a God who doesn't take away our blessings if we are ungrateful or forget to give thanks.

   Ask: Do you sometimes forget to say thank you? Why is thanksgiving important? Do you think people forget about Jesus after they get what they want? Have you ever "forgotten" to thank Jesus after you get what you want, or stopped spending time with him after your prayers were answered?

> **Closing Prayer:** *Lord, thank You for healing and forgiving us. Help us to be like the thankful leper who came back to say thank You. May we always remember to be grateful for what You do. I pray that You help us not to cause anyone to sin; instead, help us lead others to Your love and not away from it. In Your name, we pray. Amen.*

Day 18

Luke 18 – Come to Jesus

Challenge: Can anyone say the memory verse without looking it up? Repeat the memory verse as a family.

Memory Verse of the Week: *"In the same way, God's angels are happy when even one sinner turns to him"* (Luke 15:10).

> **Opening Prayer:** *Heavenly Father, thank You for listening to our prayers. You told us to never give up praying and to have childlike faith. Help us trust You and depend on You in all things. Help us to be persistent in our waiting and our noes. In Jesus's name, we pray. Amen.*

Luke 18:1-14

¹ Jesus told his disciples a story about how they should keep on praying and never give up: ² In a town there was once a judge who didn't fear God or care about people. ³ In that same town there was a widow who kept going to the judge and saying, "Make sure that I get fair treatment in court." ⁴ For a while the judge refused to do anything. Finally, he said to himself, "Even though I don't fear God or care about people, ⁵ I will help this widow because she keeps on bothering me. If I don't help her, she will wear me out." ⁶

The Lord said: Think about what that crooked judge said. ⁷ Won't God protect his chosen ones who pray to him day and night? Won't he be concerned for them? ⁸ He will surely hurry and help them. But when the Son of Man comes, will he find on this earth anyone with faith? ⁹ Jesus told a story to some people who thought they were better than others and who looked down on everyone else: ¹⁰ Two men went into the temple to pray. One was a Pharisee and the other a tax collector. ¹¹ The Pharisee stood over by himself and prayed, "God, I thank you that I am not greedy, dishonest, and unfaithful in marriage like other people. And I am really glad that I am not like that tax collector over there. ¹² I go without eating for two days a week, and I give you one tenth of all I earn." ¹³ The tax collector stood off at a distance and did not think he was good enough even to look up toward heaven. He was so sorry for what he had done that he pounded his chest and prayed, "God, have pity on me! I am such a sinner." ¹⁴ Then Jesus said, "When the two men went home, it was the tax collector and not the Pharisee who was pleasing to God. If you put yourself above others, you will be put down. But if you humble yourself, you will be honored."

Fill in the blanks as a family before you continue:

- Jesus told a story to show that we should always _____ and never give up.

Answer: (pray)

- In Jesus's story, the Pharisee bragged about his good deeds, but the tax collector humbly asked God for _____ .

Answer: (pity)

- Those who _____ themselves will be honored.

Answer: (humble)

Luke 18:15-30

[15] Some people brought their little children for Jesus to bless. But when his disciples saw them doing this, they told the people to stop bothering him. [16] So Jesus called the children over to him and said, "Let the children come to me! Don't try to stop them. People who are like these children belong to God's kingdom. [17] You will never get into God's kingdom unless you enter it like a child! [18] An important man asked Jesus, "Good Teacher, what must I do to have eternal life?" [19] Jesus said, "Why do you call me good? Only God is good. [20] You know the commandments: 'Be faithful in marriage. Do not murder. Do not steal. Do not tell lies about others. Respect your father and mother.' " [21] He told Jesus, "I have obeyed all these commandments since I was a young man." [22] When Jesus heard this, he said, "There is one thing you still need to do. Go and sell everything you own! Give the money to the poor, and you will have riches in heaven. Then come and be my follower." [23] When the man heard this, he was sad, because he was very rich. [24] Jesus saw how sad the man was. So he said, "It's terribly hard for rich people to get into God's kingdom! [25] In fact, it's easier for a camel to

go through the eye of a needle than for a rich person to get into God's kingdom." ²⁶ When the crowd heard this, they asked, "How can anyone ever be saved?" ²⁷ Jesus replied, "There are some things that people cannot do, but God can do anything." ²⁸ Peter said, "Remember, we left everything to be your followers!" ²⁹ Jesus answered, "You can be sure that anyone who gives up home or wife or brothers or family or children because of God's kingdom ³⁰ will be given much more in this life. And in the future world they will have eternal life."

Fill in the blanks as a family before you continue:

- Jesus said, "People who are like these _____ belong to God's kingdom."

Answer: (children)

- Jesus told the rich man that to have eternal life, he must sell everything he owned and give the money to the _____ .

Answer: (poor)

Luke 18:31-43

³¹ Jesus took the twelve apostles aside and said: We are now on our way to Jerusalem. Everything that the prophets wrote about the Son of Man will happen there. ³² He will be handed over to foreigners, who will make fun of him, mistreat him, and spit on him. ³³ They will beat him and kill him, but three days later he will rise to life. ³⁴ The apostles did not understand what Jesus was talking about. They could not

Luke 18 – Come to Jesus

understand, because the meaning of what he said was hidden from them. ³⁵ When Jesus was coming close to Jericho, a blind man sat begging beside the road. ³⁶ The man heard the crowd walking by and asked what was happening. ³⁷ Some people told him that Jesus from Nazareth was passing by. ³⁸ So the blind man shouted, "Jesus, Son of David, have pity on me!" ³⁹ The people who were going along with Jesus told the man to be quiet. But he shouted even louder, "Son of David, have pity on me!" ⁴⁰ Jesus stopped and told some people to bring the blind man over to him. When the blind man was getting near, Jesus asked, ⁴¹ "What do you want me to do for you?" Lord, I want to see!" he answered. ⁴² Jesus replied, "Look and you will see! Your eyes are healed because of your faith." ⁴³ At once the man could see, and he went with Jesus and started thanking God. When the crowds saw what happened, they praised God.

Fill in the blanks as a family before you continue:

- Jesus told His disciples that He would be handed over to foreigners, made fun of, beaten, and _____ .

    Answer: (killed)

- A blind man sitting beside the road shouted, "Jesus, Son of _____ , have pity on me!"

    Answer: (David)

- Jesus replied, "Look and you will see! Your eyes are _____ because of your faith."

    Answer: (healed)

Family and Kid-Friendly Questions for Discussion

1. What can we learn from the woman who kept asking the judge for help?

   Parent/Adult Tip: Jesus uses this story to show the power of persistent prayer. Let your kids know that God isn't annoyed when we pray again and again. He welcomes our faith and trust; He wants to hear from us. Think about this: If God answered every prayer in a timely manner, how often would he hear from us? It's important to teach kids that prayer isn't about saying perfect words, but about bringing your heart to God often and honestly.

   Ask: Why do you think Jesus told this story? When have you had to wait for something? What are some things we can keep praying about as a family? Have you repeated a prayer until you finally gave up on it? Or Maybe there is something that you are currently praying for? How do you feel when God doesn't answer your prayer when you want it?

2. Why did Jesus say the tax collector's prayer was better than the Pharisee's prayer?

   Parent/Adult Tip: Kids and teens are growing in self-awareness. Help them see that God is looking for humility, not pride. The definition of *humility* is a modest or low view of one's own importance, an attitude of humbleness. The Pharisee thought he was better than others, but God sees the truth in our hearts. Even when we mess up, we can be honest with God and ask for forgiveness . . . because we all mess up. Make sure kids understand that they are not better than anyone else and that we should always humble ourselves.

Ask: Can you think of a time you compared yourself to someone else or thought you were better than someone because of the clothes you had on? How do you think God wants us to treat others? What does it mean to come to God with a humble heart?

3. Why did Jesus welcome little children?

   Parent/Adult Tip: Kids need to know they are valued in God's kingdom, but even teenagers can feel overlooked or dismissed sometimes. Jesus was clear that children are not a distraction; they are an example of faith. Encourage them to come to Jesus with childlike trust. This is a good time to discuss the beauty of "childlike faith." Children depend on their parents for everything—food, shelter, love, and so on; they trust we will provide and be there. That is childlike faith, and we should depend on God in the same way. My kids think I have all the money and can get them whatever they want (which is totally not true, lol). But what if we had that same type of faith in God and really depended on him and believed he could do anything for us?

   Ask: Why do you think the disciples tried to stop the children from coming to Jesus? What makes a child's faith special? How can we come to Jesus like those children did?

4. What did Jesus tell the rich man he needed to do to follow Him?

   Parent/Adult Tip: Talk about how following Jesus often means letting go of what we hold tightly. For younger kids, it might be toys or attention. For teens, it could be a cellphone or social media. Talk about what takes up most your time. The goal is to help them see Jesus as the greatest treasure. Adults, this is a good time to share what you hold tightly. What could you let go of that's taking time away from your family and God. Let's challenge each other to fast for a day or two each week from the things we put before God, whether it is our phone, TV, social media, or our tablet.

Ask: What's something that would be hard to give up? Why do you think Jesus asked the rich young man to give up his riches? How can we show that Jesus is most important?

- Why were the disciples surprised when Jesus said it's hard for the rich to enter God's kingdom?
  Parent/Adult Tip: Our world celebrates wealth, but Jesus teaches that trusting in riches makes it harder to rely on God. This is a great chance to talk about true success and what really matters. Now, of course, having money is important, but is it the most important thing? Some families are rich in money but poor in love, or they may have poor relationships within their family, poor relationships period.

  Ask: What do you think people trust in instead of God today? Do you think having lots of money would make you happy? If you could have all the money you wanted but no family or friends, which would you choose? Do you think money can make people forget about God? What does Jesus mean when He says, "*Nothing is impossible for God*" (Luke 1:37)?

- How did people react to the blind man, and what did Jesus do instead?

Parent/Adult Tip: Talk about the importance of seeing others the way Jesus does. Sometimes, even well-meaning people can dismiss someone's needs. This is a great opportunity to build compassion for others; you never know what people are going through.

Ask: Have you seen someone being ignored or mistreated? What do you think Jesus wants us to do in those situations? How can we show love to someone who is hurting?

> **Closing Prayer:** *Lord, help our family come to You with open hearts. Teach us to pray like the tax collector, with honesty and humility and to put You first in all we do. I ask that You remove anything from our hearts and minds that is not of you and help us let go of any worldly desires, Lord. In Your name we pray. Amen.*

Day 19

Luke 19 – Jesus Loves Everyone

Challenge: Can anyone say the memory verse without looking it up? Repeat the memory verse as a family.

Memory Verse of the Week: *"In the same way, God's angels are happy when even one sinner turns to him"* (Luke 15:10).

> **Opening Prayer:** *Jesus, thank You for coming to seek and save those who are lost just like You did for Zacchaeus and me. Help our hearts be open like Yours and ready to change. I pray for strength and growth in our family and that we will follow You through good and bad times. In Your name, we pray. Amen.*

Luke 19:1-10 (GNT)

¹Jesus went on into Jericho and was passing through. ²There was a chief tax collector there named Zacchaeus, who was rich. ³He was trying to see who Jesus was, but he was a little man and could not see Jesus because of the crowd. ⁴So he ran ahead of the crowd and climbed a sycamore tree to see Jesus, who was going to pass that way. ⁵When Jesus came to that place, he looked up and said to Zacchaeus, "Hurry down, Zacchaeus, because I must stay in your house today." ⁶Zacchaeus hurried down and welcomed him with great joy. ⁷All the people who saw it started grumbling, "This man has gone as a guest to the home of a sinner!" ⁸Zacchaeus stood up and said to the Lord, "Listen, sir! I will give half my belongings to the poor, and if I have cheated anyone, I will pay back four times as much." ⁹Jesus said to him, "Salvation has come to this house today, for this man, also, is a descendant of Abraham. ¹⁰The Son of Man came to seek and to save the lost."

Luke 19 – Jesus Loves Everyone

Fill in the blanks as a family before you continue:

- Zacchaeus climbed a _____ because he wanted to see Jesus.

Answer: (tree)

- Zacchaeus promised to give to the _____ and pay back anyone he had cheated.

Answer: (poor)

Luke 19:11-27 (GNT)

[11] While the people were listening to this, Jesus continued and told them a parable. He was now almost at Jerusalem, and they supposed that the Kingdom of God was just about to appear. [12] So he said, "There was once a man of high rank who was going to a country far away to be made king, after which he planned to come back home. [13] Before he left, he called his ten servants and gave them each a gold coin and told them, 'See what you can earn with this while I am gone.' [14] Now, his own people hated him, and so they sent messengers after him to say, 'We don't want this man to be our king.' [15] "The man was made king and came back. At once he ordered his servants to appear before him, in order to find out how much they had earned. [16] The first one came and said, 'Sir, I have earned ten gold coins with the one you gave me.' [17] 'Well done,' he said; 'you are a good servant! Since you were faithful in small matters, I will put you in charge of ten cities.' [18] The second servant came and said, 'Sir, I have earned five gold coins with the one you gave me.' [19] To this

one he said, 'You will be in charge of five cities.' [20] Another servant came and said, 'Sir, here is your gold coin; I kept it hidden in a handkerchief. [21] I was afraid of you, because you are a hard man. You take what is not yours and reap what you did not plant.' [22] He said to him, 'You bad servant! I will use your own words to condemn you! You know that I am a hard man, taking what is not mine and reaping what I have not planted. [23] Well, then, why didn't you put my money in the bank? Then I would have received it back with interest when I returned.' [24] Then he said to those who were standing there, 'Take the gold coin away from him and give it to the servant who has ten coins.' [25] But they said to him, 'Sir, he already has ten coins!' [26] 'I tell you,' he replied, 'that to those who have something, even more will be given; but those who have nothing, even the little that they have will be taken away from them. [27] Now, as for those enemies of mine who did not want me to be their king, bring them here and kill them in my presence!'"

Fill in the blanks as a family before you continue:

- In the story, a man gave ten of his servants some _____ to take care of while he was gone.

Answer: (money)

- One servant earned ten times more and was given a reward to be in charge of ten _____ .

Answer: (cities)

- Another servant hid the money and didn't use it at all because he was _____ of the king.

Answer: (afraid)

Luke 19:28-48 (GNT)

[28] After Jesus said this, he went on in front of them toward Jerusalem. [29] As he came near Bethphage and Bethany at the Mount of Olives, he sent two disciples ahead [30] with these instructions: "Go to the village there ahead of you; as you go in, you will find a colt tied up that has never been ridden. Untie it and bring it here. [31] If someone asks you why you are untying it, tell him that the Master needs it." [32] They went on their way and found everything just as Jesus had told them. [33] As they were untying the colt, its owners said to them, "Why are you untying it?" [34] "The Master needs it," they answered, [35] and they took the colt to Jesus. Then they threw their cloaks over the animal and helped Jesus get on. [36] As he rode on, people spread their cloaks on the road. [37] When he came near Jerusalem, at the place where the road went down the Mount of Olives, the large crowd of his disciples began to thank God and praise him in loud voices for all the great things that they had seen: [38] "God bless the king who comes in the name of the Lord! Peace in heaven and glory to God!" [39] Then some of the Pharisees in the crowd spoke to Jesus. "Teacher," they said, "command your disciples to be quiet!" [40] Jesus answered, "I tell you that if they keep quiet, the stones themselves will start shouting." [41] He came closer to the city, and when he saw it, he wept over it, [42] saying, "If you only

knew today what is needed for peace! But now you cannot see it! ⁴³ The time will come when your enemies will surround you with barricades, blockade you, and close in on you from every side. ⁴⁴ They will completely destroy you and the people within your walls; not a single stone will they leave in its place, because you did not recognize the time when God came to save you!" ⁴⁵ Then Jesus went into the Temple and began to drive out the merchants, ⁴⁶ saying to them, "It is written in the Scriptures that God said, 'My Temple will be a house of prayer.' But you have turned it into a hideout for thieves!" ⁴⁷ Every day Jesus taught in the Temple. The chief priests, the teachers of the Law, and the leaders of the people wanted to kill him, ⁴⁸ but they could not find a way to do it, because all the people kept listening to him, not wanting to miss a single word.

Fill in the blanks as a family before you continue:

- Jesus sent two disciples to find a _____ for Him to ride into Jerusalem.

   Answer: (colt)

- As Jesus rode along, His people shouted, " God _____ the king who comes in the name of the Lord! Peace in heaven and glory to God."

   Answer: (bless)

- Some Pharisees told Jesus to make His followers stop, but He said, "If they keep quiet, the _____ will shout."

   Answer: (stones)

- Jesus went into the temple and chased out the people who were _____ instead of worshiping.

   Answer: (selling)

Family and Kid-Friendly Questions for Discussion

1. Why did Jesus ride into Jerusalem on a colt instead of a big horse?

   Parent/Adult Tip: Riding a colt or donkey showed that Jesus came in peace and humility, not as a conquering warrior like everyone expected him to be. In Jesus's time, kings rode donkeys when they came to serve and bring peace. This moment fulfilled a prophecy (Zechariah 9:9), showing that Jesus is the promised Savior.

   Ask: What does it mean that Jesus came in peace instead of power? How can we show peace in our words and actions this week? What's one way we can be humble like Jesus?

2. The people praised Jesus loudly. What are some ways we can praise Him today?

   Parent/Adult Tip: Worship isn't just singing; it's about living for God with joy. Kids and teens may not always connect with traditional praise, but they can worship through art, helping others, prayer, or gratitude. Encourage kids to express their love for God in their own way.

   Ask: How do you like to show your love for Jesus? What's one way we can worship as a family this week? Do you think it's important to thank God out loud? Why or why not?

3. Why did Jesus cry when He saw Jerusalem?

   Parent/Adult Tip: Jesus cried because the people didn't recognize God's peace. He loved them deeply and wanted them to believe and be saved. It's a beautiful picture of Jesus's heart for people, even when they turn away.

   Ask: Have you ever felt sad for someone who made a bad choice? Why do you think Jesus still loves people even when they ignore Him? How can we show love and pray for people who don't know Jesus yet?

4. Why was Jesus upset about the people selling things in the temple?

   Parent/Adult Tip: The temple was supposed to be a place of prayer and connection with God, but people were using it to make money unfairly. Jesus was protecting God's house and teaching us to honor sacred spaces.

   Ask: What does it mean to treat God's house with respect? What distractions can we remove when we pray or worship? How can we help make church or family Bible time feel special and focused on God?

5. Zacchaeus decided to give back what he stole, why do you think he did that after meeting Jesus?

   Parent/Adult Tip: When we meet Jesus, real change happens. Zacchaeus didn't just say sorry; he made things right. This is called repentance, and it's powerful. Encourage your kids to think about actions, not just words.

Luke 19 – Jesus Loves Everyone

Ask: When have you said sorry and changed something? What's a way we can make something right this week? How can Jesus help us become better and more honest people?

6. In the parable of the servants, Jesus talks about being faithful with what we're given. What are some things God has given you?

Parent/Adult Tip: Each child has unique gifts such as creativity, leadership, kindness, and responsibility. Encourage them to name and use their gifts for good. Even small things matter in God's kingdom.

Ask: What's something God has trusted you with? How can you use your gift to help someone this week? Why does God care about what we do with even the little things? Should we just sit on our gift and do nothing with it? What is the goal of the gifts with which God has blessed us?

> **Closing Prayer:** *Lord, thank You for knowing us by name and loving us even when we mess up. Help us, like Zacchaeus, to live differently after meeting You; Help us be transformed and become a new creation. May our home be filled with joy and transformation for the rest of our lives. In Your name, we pray. Amen.*

Day 20

Luke 20 – Listening to Jesus

Challenge: Can anyone say the memory verse without looking it up? Repeat the memory verse as a family.

Memory Verse of the Week: *"In the same way, God's angels are happy when even one sinner turns to him"* (Luke 15:10).

> **Opening Prayer:** *Heavenly Father, in today's Scripture passage, Jesus answered hard questions and stood strong in truth. Help our family be wise, kind, and full of Your truth. Teach us to stand for what is right and give us the courage and boldness to step out for Jesus always. In Jesus's name we pray. Amen.*

Luke 20:1-19

¹ One day, Jesus was teaching in the temple and telling the good news. So the chief priests, the teachers, and the nation's leaders ² asked him, "What right do you have to do these things? Who gave you this authority?" ³ Jesus replied, "I want to ask you a question. ⁴ Who gave John the right to baptize? Was it God in heaven or merely some human being?" ⁵ They talked this over and said to each other, "We can't say God gave John this right. Jesus will ask us why we

didn't believe John. ⁶ And we can't say it was merely some human who gave John the right to baptize. The crowd will stone us to death, because they think John was a prophet." ⁷ So they told Jesus, "We don't know who gave John the right to baptize." ⁸ Jesus replied, "Then I won't tell you who gave me the right to do what I do." ⁹ Jesus told the people this story: A man once planted a vineyard and rented it out. Then he left the country for a long time. ¹⁰ When it was time to harvest the crop, he sent a servant to ask the renters for his share of the grapes. But they beat up the servant and sent him away without anything. ¹¹ So the owner sent another servant. The renters also beat him up. They insulted him terribly and sent him away without a thing. ¹² The owner sent a third servant. He was also beaten terribly and thrown out of the vineyard. ¹³ The owner then said to himself, "What am I going to do? I know what. I'll send my son, the one I love so much. They will surely respect him!" ¹⁴ When the renters saw the owner's son, they said to one another, "Someday he will own the vineyard. Let's kill him! Then we can have it all for ourselves." ¹⁵ So they threw him out of the vineyard and killed him. Jesus asked, "What do you think the owner of the vineyard will do? ¹⁶ I'll tell you what. He will come and kill those renters and let someone else have his vineyard." When the people heard this, they said, "This must never happen!" ¹⁷ But Jesus looked straight at them and said, "Then what do the Scriptures mean when they say, 'The stone the builders tossed aside is now the most important stone of all'? ¹⁸ Anyone who stumbles over this stone will get hurt, and anyone it falls on will be smashed to pieces." ¹⁹ The chief priests and the teachers of the Law of Moses knew that Jesus was talking about them when he was telling this story. They wanted to arrest him right then, but they were afraid of the people.

Fill in the blanks as a family before you continue:

- The religious leaders questioned Jesus's _____ to teach and do miracles because they didn't want to believe He was from God.

   Answer: (authority)

- Jesus told a story about a vineyard to show how people had rejected God's _____ , including His own Son.

   Answer: (messengers)

- The stone the builders rejected has become the most important _____ .

   Answer: (stone)

Luke 20:20-40

[20] Jesus' enemies kept watching him closely, because they wanted to hand him over to the Roman governor. So they sent some men who pretended to be good. But they were really spies trying to catch Jesus saying something wrong. [21] The spies said to him, "Teacher, we know you teach the truth about what God wants people to do. And you treat everyone with the same respect, no matter who they are. [22] Tell us, should we pay taxes to the Emperor or not?" [23] Jesus knew they were trying to trick him. So he told them, [24] "Show me

a coin." Then he asked, "Whose picture and name are on it?" "The Emperor's," they answered. ²⁵ Then he told them, "Give the Emperor what belongs to him and give God what belongs to God." ²⁶ Jesus' enemies could not catch him saying anything wrong there in front of the people. They were amazed at his answer and kept quiet. ²⁷ The Sadducees did not believe that people would rise to life after death. So some of them came to Jesus ²⁸ and said: Teacher, Moses wrote that if a married man dies and has no children, his brother should marry the widow. Their first son would then be thought of as the son of the dead brother. ²⁹ There were once seven brothers. The first one married, but died without having any children. ³⁰ The second one married his brother's widow, and he also died without having any children. ³¹ The same thing happened to the third one. Finally, all seven brothers married this woman and died without having any children. ³² At last the woman died. ³³ When God raises people from death, whose wife will this woman be? All seven brothers had married her. ³⁴ Jesus answered: The people in this world get married. ³⁵ But in the future world no one who is worthy to rise from death will either marry ³⁶ or die. They will be like the angels and will be God's children, because they have been raised to life. ³⁷ In the story about the burning bush, Moses clearly shows that people will live again. He said, "The Lord is the God worshiped by Abraham, Isaac, and Jacob." ³⁸ So the Lord isn't the God of the dead, but of the living. This means that everyone is alive as far as God is concerned. ³⁹ Some of the teachers of the Law of Moses said, "Teacher, you have given a good answer!" ⁴⁰ From then on, no one dared to ask Jesus any questions.

Fill in the blanks as a family before you continue:

- Jesus told the spies, "Give the Emperor what belongs to him and give _____ what belongs to God."

    Answer: (God)

- Jesus reminded everyone that God is not the God of the dead but of the _____ .

    Answer: (living)

- In heaven, people will not _____ or be given in marriage, but will be like the angels.

    Answer: (marry)

Luke 20:41-47

⁴¹ Jesus asked, "Why do people say that the Messiah will be the son of King David? ⁴² In the book of Psalms, David himself says, 'The Lord said to my Lord, Sit at my right side ⁴³ until I make your enemies into a footstool for you.' ⁴⁴ David spoke of the Messiah as his Lord, so how can the Messiah be his son?" ⁴⁵ While everyone was listening to Jesus, he said to his disciples: ⁴⁶ Guard against the teachers of the Law of Moses! They love to walk around in long robes, and they like to be greeted in the market. They want the front seats in the synagogues and the best seats at banquets. ⁴⁷ But they cheat widows out of their homes and then pray long prayers just to show off. These teachers will be punished most of all.

Fill in the blanks as a family before you continue:

- Jesus asked why people say the _____ is David's son if David called Him Lord.

    Answer: (Messiah)

- Jesus warned the people to beware of the _____ , who like to show off and take advantage of others.

    Answer: (teachers of the Law)

Family and Kid-Friendly Questions for Discussion

1. What does the parable of the vineyard teach us about listening to God?

    Parent/Adult Tip: In this parable, the landowner represents God, and the farmers represent people who rejected His messengers, and eventually His Son, Jesus. Talk about what it means to treat others with respect and to obey those who care for us, such as parents, family members, and other adults we are around. Discuss how we sometimes reject God's messages when they challenge our comfort. Parents/Adults, this is a good time to discuss times we have rejected God's message or have been disobedient. Share how your disobedience led to an unsatisfactory outcome because we wanted to do something that was easier than what God wanted us to do. Emphasize how God's love is patient but also calls for response. We do not want to be like the farmers in the parable.

    Ask: Who do you think the landowner represents in this story? What about the son? Why do you think the farmers acted the way they did? Have you ever ignored advice that was meant to help you only to discover that you should have taken the advice? What happened? How can we listen and respond when God speaks to us, even if it's not easy?

2. What can we learn from Jesus's answer about paying taxes to the Emperor (i.e., Caesar)?

   Parent/Adult Tip: Use this as a chance to talk about honoring both God and the responsibilities we have in the world. This parable is not just about paying taxes but following rules that we have in society. Jesus wants us to be model citizens of this world and of the kingdom of heaven; talk about the differences between the two. Talk about how you can do both. Even kids and teens can be responsible with their time, words, and resources. We can praise and worship God, love others, and be kind for God's kingdom even as follow the rules of the place where we live.

   Ask: What are some things that belong to God in your life (e.g., time, talents, kindness)? How can we "give to God" with our lives? Why do you think Jesus didn't just say, "Don't pay taxes"?

3. What did Jesus say about life after death?

   Parent/Adult Tip: This can be an emotional topic. Explain gently that Jesus reminds us that death isn't the end for believers. We can live forever with Him. How amazing is that!? Let your children express any fears or questions they have without rushing to answer everything. Explain to your children that when we have a relationship with God, know his word, and love him, death is not the end for us. This gives us hope and makes us realize how good and loving God really is. I mentioned this earlier, but someone told me that the only thing we can take to Heaven is our children. Let's love and learn more about Jesus, so we can all be together again!

Ask: What do you imagine Heaven might be like? How does knowing Jesus loves you forever make you feel? What can we do to have a relationship with Jesus? What do you think it means to be "alive with God"?

4. How can we keep our faith real, not just something we act out?

    Parent/Adult Tip: Talk about how faith is not a costume or a Sunday thing; it's a daily relationship with Jesus. Ask your kids to think about what "real faith" looks like at school, with friends, and at home. Model this by sharing your own efforts and growth areas. Assure kids that we are prone to fail sometimes, but God wants to see how we respond in those failures. He knows our hearts and loves us. Parents/Adults, discuss and give examples. Come up with a daily goal as a family. In my family we like to "huddle up" in the morning (sporty family): We come together, each person prays, and then we "break out" with a "Thank you, Jesus!" on the count of three. It could be something as simple as that.

    Ask: When is it hardest for you to act like Jesus? What helps you stay strong in your faith even when others are failing to do so? How can we support each other as a family in living out our faith every day?

Closing Prayer: *God, thank You for Jesus's courage and wisdom. May our family always listen to Your Word and live in a way that honors You. Help us to hear from You and know Your voice better as we continue to grow and spend more time with You, Lord. We love You, Jesus. In Your name, we pray. Amen.*

Day 21

Luke 21 – Jesus Is Coming Again

Challenge: Can anyone say the memory verse without looking it up? Repeat the memory verse as a family.

Memory Verse of the Week: *"In the same way, God's angels are happy when even one sinner turns to him"* (Luke 15:10).

Opening Prayer: *Father God, help us not be afraid of the future, but stay close to You and keep our faith strong. Jesus talked about things to come and told us to stay alert and trust Him. I pray my family's faith and trust continues to grow, so when storms come our way, Lord, we will not be shaken because our foundation is built on You. In Jesus's name, we pray. Amen.*

Luke 21 – Jesus Is Coming Again

Luke 21:1-19 (GNT)

¹ Jesus looked around and saw rich people dropping their gifts in the Temple treasury, ² and he also saw a very poor widow dropping in two little copper coins. ³ He said, "I tell you that this poor widow put in more than all the others. ⁴ For the others offered their gifts from what they had to spare of their riches; but she, poor as she is, gave all she had to live on." ⁵ Some of the disciples were talking about the Temple, how beautiful it looked with its fine stones and the gifts offered to God. Jesus said, ⁶ "All this you see—the time will come when not a single stone here will be left in its place; every one will be thrown down." ⁷ "Teacher," they asked, "when will this be? And what will happen in order to show that the time has come for it to take place?" ⁸ Jesus said, "Watch out; don't be fooled. Many men, claiming to speak for me, will come and say, 'I am he!' and, 'The time has come!' But don't follow them. ⁹ Don't be afraid when you hear of wars and revolutions; such things must happen first, but they do not mean that the end is near." ¹⁰ He went on to say, "Countries will fight each other; kingdoms will attack one another. ¹¹ There will be terrible earthquakes, famines, and plagues everywhere; there will be strange and terrifying things coming from the sky. ¹² Before all these things take place, however, you will be arrested and persecuted; you will be handed over to be tried in synagogues and be put in prison; you will be brought before kings and rulers for my sake. ¹³ This will be your chance to tell the Good News. ¹⁴ Make up your minds ahead of time not to worry about how you will defend yourselves, ¹⁵ because I will give you such words

and wisdom that none of your enemies will be able to refute or contradict what you say. ¹⁶ You will be handed over by your parents, your brothers, your relatives, and your friends; and some of you will be put to death. ¹⁷ Everyone will hate you because of me. ¹⁸ But not a single hair from your heads will be lost. ¹⁹ Stand firm, and you will save yourselves.

Fill in the blanks as a family before you continue:

- The poor widow gave _____ than the rich people because she gave all she had, and the rich gave what they _____ need.

    Answer: (more, didn't)

- Jesus warned His followers not to be fooled by people claiming to be Him. "Many . . . will come and say, 'I am _____ !' and 'The time has come!' But don't _____ them."

    Answer: (He, follow)

- Jesus said His followers would be hated and even arrested, but He promised to give them the _____ to know what to say.

    Answer: (wisdom)

Luke 21:20-38 (GNT)

²⁰ "When you see Jerusalem surrounded by armies, then you will know that it will soon be destroyed. ²¹ Then those who are in Judea must run away to the hills; those who are in the city must leave, and those who are out in the country must

not go into the city. ²² For those will be 'The Days of Punishment,' to make come true all that the Scriptures say. ²³ How terrible it will be in those days for women who are pregnant and for mothers with little babies! Terrible distress will come upon this land, and God's punishment will fall on this people. ²⁴ Some will be killed by the sword, and others will be taken as prisoners to all countries; and the heathen will trample over Jerusalem until their time is up. ²⁵ "There will be strange things happening to the sun, the moon, and the stars. On earth whole countries will be in despair, afraid of the roar of the sea and the raging tides. ²⁶ People will faint from fear as they wait for what is coming over the whole earth, for the powers in space will be driven from their courses. ²⁷ Then the Son of Man will appear, coming in a cloud with great power and glory. ²⁸ When these things begin to happen, stand up and raise your heads, because your salvation is near." ²⁹ Then Jesus told them this parable: "Think of the fig tree and all the other trees. ³⁰ When you see their leaves beginning to appear, you know that summer is near. ³¹ In the same way, when you see these things happening, you will know that the Kingdom of God is about to come. ³² "Remember that all these things will take place before the people now living have all died. ³³ Heaven and earth will pass away, but my words will never pass away.³⁴ "Be careful not to let yourselves become occupied with too much feasting and drinking and with the worries of this life, or that Day may suddenly catch you ³⁵ like a trap. For it will come upon all people everywhere on earth. ³⁶ Be on watch and pray always that you will have the strength to go safely through all those things that will happen and to stand before the Son of Man." ³⁷ Jesus spent those days teaching in the Temple, and when evening came, he would go out and spend the night on the Mount of Olives. [38] Early each morning all the people went to the Temple to listen to him.

Fill in the blanks as a family before you continue:

- Jesus warned that when Jerusalem is surrounded by armies, it will soon be completely _____ .

Answer: (destroyed)

- Watch out and keep _____ that you can escape all that is going to happen and that the Son of Man will be pleased with you.

Answer: (praying)

Family and Kid-Friendly Questions for Discussion

1. Why did Jesus say the poor widow gave more than the rich people?

    Parent/Adult Tip: Teach your children that Jesus sees the heart behind the gift, not just how much is given. This is a chance to talk about generosity, trust, and sacrificial giving, even when it's a small amount. Younger kids might understand this with a story or a toy as an example. Older kids can explore the concept of giving joyfully and selflessly. Let's take this time to think about something we can give, whether it's donating a toy or donating our time to volunteer. Talk about how the widow trusted God with **all** she had whereas the rich people gave what they didn't need, so it was easy for them to give.

Ask: Why do you think Jesus said her gift was the greatest? What are some small but meaningful ways we can give to others (e.g., time, kindness, or prayer)? Have you ever shared something even when it was hard?

2. Jesus told His followers not to be fooled. How do we avoid being tricked today?

   Parent/Adult Tip: This is a great time to talk about truth versus lies, especially online or from peer pressure. Teach them the truth of what God says about them and to compare everything said about them to God's Word. Teenagers might need extra help to recognize cultural messages that don't align with Jesus. Encourage your children to know and trust in their identity in Christ:

   I Am Loved: Use this truth when you feel lonely or unimportant.

   God's Truth: You are deeply loved, not because of what you do, but because of who you are. God's love never runs out.

   "*I have loved you with an everlasting love* (Jeremiah 31:3 NIV).

   I Am God's Child: Use this truth when you feel left out or need comfort.

   God's Truth: You are not alone; you belong to God's family. You can call God "Father" and know He cares for you.

   "*God's Spirit doesn't make us slaves who are afraid of him. Instead, we become his children and call him our Father*" Romans 8:15

I Am Forgiven: Use this truth when you feel guilty or ashamed.

God's Truth: No mistake is too big for God. When you're honest with Him, He gives you a clean heart.

"If we confess our sins to God, he can always be trusted to forgive us and take our sins away" (1 John 1:9).

I Am Chosen: Use this truth when you feel like you don't matter.

God's Truth: God picked you on purpose. He gave you a mission to love, help, and shine His light.

"You did not choose me. I chose you and sent you out to produce fruit, the kind of fruit that will last" (John 15:16).

I Am Strong in Christ: Use this truth when you feel weak, tired, or scared.

God's Truth: Even when life is hard, you can be strong because Jesus lives in you.

"Christ gives me the strength to face anything" (Philippians 4:13).

Ask: What are some things people might say that sound true but aren't? How can we check whether something lines up with what Jesus taught? Who can we talk to when we're not sure what to believe?

3. Why did Jesus say not to panic when scary things happen?

   Parent/Adult Tip: Life can be uncertain, but Jesus promises peace. Use this to talk about trusting God in scary times, whether it's a storm, illness, drama with friends, or world events. Share

Luke 21 – Jesus Is Coming Again

about times that your family has seen God help you stay calm and strong.

Ask: What are some things that scare you? What can we do together when we feel worried? How does trusting Jesus help you feel safe? *"Don't be afraid. I am with you"* (Isaiah 41:10).

4. Jesus said, "You will be saved by being faithful to me" (Luke 21:19). What does that mean?

   Parent/Adult Tip: Jesus wasn't promising that we would not have any trouble; He was promising His care and eternal protection. As Christians, this is a good time with talk to our kids and let them know we are not exempt from pain or trouble; things will be hard in life. But even in trouble, God sees us, knows us, and has a forever plan for us.

   Ask: What does it mean to know God watches over every part of your life? Can you think of a time you felt God taking care of you? What helps you feel safe and loved by God?

5. Why did Jesus go to pray every night?

   Parent/Adult Tip: Throughout the book of Luke, prayer is a major theme. You may have noticed we have discussed prayer a lot; that's because prayer is a must. Make sure to discuss that prayer should be part of our relationship with God, not just some words we recite every night. Even Jesus needed to spend time with God, His Father. Prayer isn't just about asking; it's about listening, thanking, and being close to our Father. Encourage your kids to see prayer as friendship time with God, not as a chore.

Ask: Why do you think Jesus prayed so often? What's something you'd like to pray about today? What's your favorite way to connect with God (e.g., writing, singing, walking, or talking)?

Challenge: Let's take five minutes and write a letter to God.

> **Closing Prayer:** *Lord, thank You that no matter what happens in the world, no matter who is president, and no matter what may come our way, You are in control. Help us to keep watching, praying, and trusting in You as a family. Give our family self-control and discipline to follow your Word. In Your name, we pray. Amen.*

Day 22

Luke 22 – The Last Supper

Challenge: Can anyone say the memory verse without looking it up? Repeat the memory verse as a family.

Memory Verse of the Week: "*In the same way, God's angels are happy when even one sinner turns to him*" (Luke 15:10).

Luke 22 – The Last Supper

> **Opening Prayer:** *Jesus, as we read today, help us feel the love You showed at the Last Supper and in the garden. You knew what was coming, but You still chose the cross for us. Thank You for that love. In Your name, we pray. Amen.*

Luke 22:1-13

¹ The Festival of Thin Bread, also called Passover, was near. ² The chief priests and the teachers of the Law of Moses were looking for a way to get rid of Jesus, because they were afraid of what the people might do. ³ Then Satan entered the heart of Judas Iscariot, who was one of the twelve apostles. ⁴ Judas went to talk with the chief priests and the officers of the temple police about how he could help them arrest Jesus. ⁵ They were very pleased and offered to pay Judas some money. ⁶ He agreed and started looking for a good chance to betray Jesus when the crowds were not around. ⁷ The day had come for the Festival of Thin Bread, and it was time to kill the Passover lambs. ⁸ So Jesus said to Peter and John, "Go and prepare the Passover meal for us to eat." ⁹ But they asked, "Where do you want us to prepare it?" ¹⁰ Jesus told them, "As you go into the city, you will meet a man carrying a jar of water. Follow him into the house ¹¹ and say to the owner, 'Our teacher wants to know where he can eat the Passover meal with his disciples.' ¹² The owner will take you upstairs and show you a large room ready for you to use. Prepare the meal there." ¹³ Peter and John left. They found

everything just as Jesus had told them, and they prepared the Passover meal.

Fill in the blanks as a family before you continue:

- The Festival of _____ Bread was about to begin, and the religious leaders were looking for a way to kill Jesus.

    Answer: (Thin)

- Judas went to the chief priests and agreed to _____ Jesus for money.

    Answer: (betray)

- Jesus told Peter and John to prepare the _____ meal in a house where they would find a room already ready.

    Answer: (Passover)

Luke 22:14-30

¹⁴ When the time came for Jesus and the apostles to eat, ¹⁵ he said to them, "I have very much wanted to eat this Passover meal with you before I suffer. ¹⁶ I tell you I will not eat another Passover meal until it is finally eaten in God's kingdom." ¹⁷ Jesus took a cup of wine in his hands and gave thanks to God. Then he told the apostles, "Take this wine and share it with each other. ¹⁸ I tell you that I will not drink any more wine until God's kingdom comes." ¹⁹ Jesus took some bread in his hands and gave thanks for it. He broke the bread and handed it to his apostles. Then he said, "This is my body, which is given for you. Eat this as a way of remembering

me!" ²⁰ After the meal he took another cup of wine in his hands. Then he said, "This is my blood. It is poured out for you, and with it God makes his new agreement. ²¹ The one who will betray me is here at the table with me! ²² The Son of Man will die in the way that has been decided for him, but it will be terrible for the one who betrays him!" ²³ Then the apostles started arguing about who would ever do such a thing. ²⁴ The apostles got into an argument about which one of them was the greatest. ²⁵ So Jesus told them: Foreign kings order their people around, and powerful rulers call themselves everyone's friends. ²⁶ But don't be like them. The most important one of you should be like the least important, and your leader should be like a servant. ²⁷ Who do people think is the greatest, a person who is served or one who serves? Isn't it the one who is served? But I have been with you as a servant. ²⁸ You have stayed with me in all my troubles. ²⁹ So I will give you the right to rule as kings, just as my Father has given me the right to rule as a king. ³⁰ You will eat and drink with me in my kingdom, and you will each sit on a throne to judge the twelve tribes of Israel.

Fill in the blanks as a family before you continue:

- Jesus broke the _____ with His disciples and said it was His body given for them.

Answer: (bread)

- Jesus said the cup was the new _____ because of His blood poured out for them.

Answer: (agreement)

- Jesus taught that the greatest person is the one who _____ others, not the one who is served.

Answer: (serves)

Luke 22:31-46

³¹ Jesus said, "Simon, listen to me! Satan has demanded the right to test each one of you, as a farmer does when he separates wheat from the husks. ³² But Simon, I have prayed that your faith will be strong. And when you have come back to me, help the others." ³³ Peter said, "Lord, I am ready to go with you to jail and even to die with you." ³⁴ Jesus replied, "Peter, I tell you that before a rooster crows tomorrow morning, you will say three times that you don't know me." ³⁵ Jesus asked his disciples, "When I sent you out without a moneybag or a traveling bag or sandals, did you need anything?" "No!" they answered. ³⁶ Jesus told them, "But now, if you have a moneybag, take it with you. Also take a traveling bag, and if you don't have a sword, sell some of your clothes and buy one. ³⁷ Do this because the Scriptures say, 'He was considered a criminal.' This was written about me, and it will soon come true." ³⁸ The disciples said, "Lord, here are two swords!" "Enough of that!" Jesus replied. ³⁹ Jesus went out to the Mount of Olives, as he often did, and his disciples went with him. ⁴⁰ When they got there, he told them, "Pray that you won't be tested." ⁴¹ Jesus walked on a little way before he knelt down and prayed, ⁴² "Father, if you will, please don't make me suffer by drinking from this cup. But do what you want, and not what I want." ⁴³ Then an angel from heaven came to help him. ⁴⁴ Jesus was in great pain and prayed so

sincerely that his sweat fell to the ground like drops of blood. ⁴⁵ Jesus got up from praying and went over to his disciples. They were asleep and worn out from being so sad. ⁴⁶ He said to them, "Why are you asleep? Wake up and pray that you won't be tested."

Fill in the blanks as a family before you continue:

- Jesus told Peter that he would say three times that he didn't even _____ Him.

Answer: (know)

- Jesus went to the Mount of Olives to _____ and asked His disciples to pray too.

Answer: (pray)

- Jesus was so full of sorrow that He prayed with all His heart, and His sweat was like drops of _____ .

Answer: (blood)

Luke 22:47-71

⁴⁷ While Jesus was still speaking, a crowd came up. It was led by Judas, one of the twelve apostles. He went over to Jesus and greeted him with a kiss. ⁴⁸ Jesus asked Judas, "Are you betraying the Son of Man with a kiss?" ⁴⁹ When Jesus' disciples saw what was about to happen, they asked, "Lord, should we attack them with a sword?" ⁵⁰ One of the disciples even struck at the high priest's servant with his sword and cut off the servant's right ear. ⁵¹ "Enough of that!" Jesus

said. Then he touched the servant's ear and healed it. ⁵² Jesus spoke to the chief priests, the temple police, and the leaders who had come to arrest him. He said, "Why do you come out with swords and clubs and treat me like a criminal? ⁵³ I was with you every day in the temple, and you didn't arrest me. But this is your time, and darkness is in control." ⁵⁴ Jesus was arrested and led away to the house of the high priest, while Peter followed at a distance. ⁵⁵ Some people built a fire in the middle of the courtyard and were sitting around it. Peter sat there with them, ⁵⁶ and a servant girl saw him. Then after she had looked at him carefully, she said, "This man was with Jesus!" ⁵⁷ Peter said, "Woman, I don't even know that man!" ⁵⁸ A little later someone else saw Peter and said, "You are one of them!" "No, I'm not!" Peter replied. ⁵⁹ About an hour later another man insisted, "This man must have been with Jesus. They both come from Galilee." ⁶⁰ Peter replied, "I don't know what you are talking about!" Right then, while Peter was still speaking, a rooster crowed. ⁶¹ The Lord turned and looked at Peter. And Peter remembered that the Lord had said, "Before a rooster crows tomorrow morning, you will say three times that you don't know me." ⁶² Then Peter went out and cried bitterly. ⁶³ The men who were guarding Jesus made fun of him and beat him. ⁶⁴ They put a blindfold on him and said, "Tell us who struck you!" ⁶⁵ They kept on insulting Jesus in many other ways. ⁶⁶ At daybreak the nation's leaders, the chief priests, and the teachers of the Law of Moses got together and brought Jesus before their council. ⁶⁷ They said, "Tell us! Are you the Messiah Jesus replied, "If I said so, you wouldn't believe me. ⁶⁸ And if I asked you a question, you wouldn't answer. ⁶⁹ But from now on, the Son of Man will be seated at the right side of God All-Powerful." [70] Then they asked, "Are you the Son of God?" Jesus answered, "You say I am!" [71] They replied, "Why do we need more witnesses? He said it himself!"

Fill in the blanks as a family before you continue:

- Judas showed the soldiers who Jesus was by giving Him a _____ .

  Answer: (kiss)

- One of the disciples cut off a servant's _____ , but Jesus healed him.

  Answer: (ear)

- Peter denied knowing Jesus _____ times, just like Jesus had said he would.

  Answer: (three)

- The leaders asked Jesus if He was the Son of God, and Jesus said, "You say I _____ ."

  Answer: (Am)

Family and Kid-Friendly Questions for Discussion

1. Why did Jesus want to celebrate the Passover with His disciples before He died?

   Parent/Adult Tip: The Passover meal reminded God's people of how He rescued them from slavery in Egypt. Jesus gave this tradition even more meaning by pointing to His own sacrifice. Use this moment to talk about how Jesus prepares for his crucifixion by spending his last night with his disciples sharing a meal and demonstrating that He loves us deeply.

Ask: Why do you think special meals help us remember important things? How do you feel knowing Jesus wanted to spend time with His friends before dying? How can we make our meals together more meaningful?

2. How does it feel to know that Jesus served others, even though He's the Son of God?

    Parent/Adult Tip: Jesus could have demanded praise but chose to be humble. Jesus was the perfect example of what a leader should be. Serving shows love, and Jesus leads us by example. Parents/Adults, how can we do better and be more of the leader Jesus is? Talk about how being great in God's eyes means helping others, not bossing them around.

    Ask: Can you think of a time someone served you kindly? How did it feel? What's one way you can serve someone in your family this week? Why is it sometimes hard to serve others?

3. Why do you think Judas chose to betray Jesus?

    Parent/Adult Tip: Judas was tempted by money and gave into temptation to sin. Use this time to talk honestly about temptation and how God always gives us a way out. Reassure your kids that even when we mess up, Jesus is ready to forgive if we turn to Him.

Ask: Have you ever done something you knew was wrong because you felt tempted? What helps you make better choices when you feel pressured? How do you think Jesus felt knowing that Judas had betrayed Him?

4. What did Jesus mean when He said, "Pray that you won't be tested"?

   Parent/Adult Tip: Jesus knew His followers were about to go through something hard. Prayer gives us strength before challenges hit. Help your kids see prayer as something powerful, not just words. Prayer is the equivalent of working out physically, except it is getting your mind and heart stronger.

   Ask: When is a good time to pray—when we're in trouble or before? What do you pray about when you're scared or nervous? How can we build the habit of prayer as a family?

5. How do you think Peter felt after he denied Jesus three times?

   Parent/Adult Tip: Peter loved Jesus, but he messed up. Focus on the idea that mistakes don't define us, God's forgiveness does. Encourage kids not to hide from God when they mess up.

   Ask: Have you ever made a mistake and felt really bad afterward? What does it mean that Jesus forgave Peter and still used him in big ways? How do we show others forgiveness like Jesus did?

6. What does it mean to follow Jesus even when it's difficult?

   Parent/Adult Tip: Faith isn't always easy. Help your child understand that Jesus walks with us through the hard stuff. Let them know it's okay to ask questions and lean on God during tough times.

Ask: What's hard about being a Christian at school or with friends? How can our family help each other stay strong in faith? What can we do when we feel like giving up?

> **Closing Prayer:** *Lord, thank You for loving us even when it cost You everything. Help us to follow You closely and remember Your sacrifice with thankful hearts daily. Keep our family united in Your love. We cannot say thank you enough for this sacrifice and for Your blood that was shed. In Your name, we pray. Amen.*

Day 23

Luke 23 - Jesus Dies for Us

Challenge: Can anyone say the memory verse without looking it up? Repeat the memory verse as a family.

Memory Verse of the Week: "*In the same way, God's angels are happy when even one sinner turns to him*" (Luke 15:10).

Luke 23 – Jesus Dies for Us

> **Opening Prayer:** *King Jesus, we see how much You suffered to save us. Help our family to slow down and remember that You died because You love us. We are so grateful. Continue to help us grow in Your love each day. In Your name, we pray. Amen.*

Luke 23:1-12 (GNT)

¹ The whole group rose up and took Jesus before Pilate, ² where they began to accuse him: "We caught this man misleading our people, telling them not to pay taxes to the Emperor and claiming that he himself is the Messiah, a king." ³ Pilate asked him, "Are you the king of the Jews?" "So you say," answered Jesus. ⁴ Then Pilate said to the chief priests and the crowds, "I find no reason to condemn this man." ⁵ But they insisted even more strongly, "With his teaching he is starting a riot among the people all through Judea. He began in Galilee and now has come here." ⁶ When Pilate heard this, he asked, "Is this man a Galilean?" ⁷ When he learned that Jesus was from the region ruled by Herod, he sent him to Herod, who was also in Jerusalem at that time. ⁸ Herod was very pleased when he saw Jesus, because he had heard about him and had been wanting to see him for a long time. He was hoping to see Jesus perform some miracle. ⁹ So Herod asked Jesus many questions, but Jesus made no answer. ¹⁰ The chief priests and the teachers of the Law stepped forward and made strong accusations against Jesus. ¹¹ Herod and his soldiers made fun of Jesus and treated him with contempt; then they put a fine robe on him and

sent him back to Pilate. ¹² On that very day Herod and Pilate became friends; before this they had been enemies.

Fill in the blanks as a family before you continue:

- When Jesus was sent to Herod, He did not _____, even though He was being questioned and mocked.

Answer: (answer)

- Pilate and Herod had been enemies before, but after meeting about Jesus, they became _____.

Answer: (friends)

Luke 23:13-43 (GNT)

¹³ Pilate called together the chief priests, the leaders, and the people, ¹⁴ and said to them, "You brought this man to me and said that he was misleading the people. Now, I have examined him here in your presence, and I have not found him guilty of any of the crimes you accuse him of. ¹⁵ Nor did Herod find him guilty, for he sent him back to us. There is nothing this man has done to deserve death. ¹⁶ So I will have him whipped and let him go." ¹⁷ ¹⁸ The whole crowd cried out, "Kill him! Set Barabbas free for us!" (¹⁹ Barabbas had been put in prison for a riot that had taken place in the city, and for murder.) ²⁰ Pilate wanted to set Jesus free, so he appealed to the crowd again. ²¹ But they shouted back, "Crucify him! Crucify him!" ²² Pilate said to them the third time, "But what crime has he committed? I cannot find anything he has done to deserve death! I will have him whipped and

set him free." ²³ But they kept on shouting at the top of their voices that Jesus should be crucified, and finally their shouting succeeded. ²⁴ So Pilate passed the sentence on Jesus that they were asking for. ²⁵ He set free the man they wanted, the one who had been put in prison for riot and murder, and he handed Jesus over for them to do as they wished. ²⁶ The soldiers led Jesus away, and as they were going, they met a man from Cyrene named Simon who was coming into the city from the country. They seized him, put the cross on him, and made him carry it behind Jesus. ²⁷ A large crowd of people followed him; among them were some women who were weeping and wailing for him. ²⁸ Jesus turned to them and said, "Women of Jerusalem! Don't cry for me, but for yourselves and your children. ²⁹ For the days are coming when people will say, 'How lucky are the women who never had children, who never bore babies, who never nursed them!' ³⁰ That will be the time when people will say to the mountains, 'Fall on us!' and to the hills, 'Hide us!' ³¹ For if such things as these are done when the wood is green, what will happen when it is dry? ³² Two other men, both of them criminals, were also led out to be put to death with Jesus. ³³ When they came to the place called "The Skull," they crucified Jesus there, and the two criminals, one on his right and the other on his left. ³⁴ Jesus said, "Forgive them, Father! They don't know what they are doing."They divided his clothes among themselves by throwing dice. ³⁵ The people stood there watching while the Jewish leaders made fun of him: "He saved others; let him save himself if he is the Messiah whom God has chosen!" ³⁶ The soldiers also made fun of him: they came up to him and offered him cheap wine, ³⁷ and said, "Save yourself if you are the king of the Jews!" [38] Above him were written these words: "This is the King of the Jews." [39] One of the criminals hanging there hurled insults at him: "Aren't you the Messiah? Save yourself and us!" [40] The other one, however, rebuked him, saying, "Don't you fear God? You received the same sentence he did. [41] Ours, however, is only right, because we are getting what we deserve for what we did; but he has done no wrong." [42] And he said to Jesus, "Remember me, Jesus, when you come as King!"[43] Jesus said to him, "I promise you that today you will be in Paradise with me."

Fill in the blanks as a family before you continue:

- Pilate wanted to let Jesus go, but the people kept shouting "_____ Him!"

    Answer: (cross)

- Instead of Jesus, the crowd chose to set free a man who was guilty of _____.

    Answer: (murder)

- As Jesus was nailed to the cross, He asked God to _____ the people who were hurting Him.

    Answer: (forgive)

- One of the criminals on the cross made fun of Jesus, but the other one asked Jesus to remember him when He comes as _____.

    Answer: (king)

Luke 23:44-56 (GNT)

44-45 It was about twelve o'clock when the sun stopped shining and darkness covered the whole country until three o'clock; and the curtain hanging in the Temple was torn in two. ⁴⁶ Jesus cried out in a loud voice, "Father! In your hands I place my spirit!" He said this and died. ⁴⁷ The army officer saw what had happened, and he praised God, saying, "Certainly he was a good man!"⁴⁸ When the people who had gathered there to watch the spectacle saw what happened, they all went back home, beating their breasts in sorrow. ⁴⁹ All those who knew Jesus personally, including the women who had followed him from Galilee, stood at a distance to watch.⁵⁰⁻⁵¹ There was a man named Joseph from Arimathea, a town in Judea. He was a good and honorable man, who was waiting for the coming of the Kingdom of God. Although he was a member of the Council, he had not agreed with their decision and action. ⁵² He went into the presence of Pilate and asked for the body of Jesus. ⁵³ Then he took the body down, wrapped it in a linen sheet, and placed it in a tomb which had been dug out of solid rock and which had never been used. ⁵⁴ It was Friday, and the Sabbath was about to begin.⁵⁵ The women who had followed Jesus from Galilee went with Joseph and saw the tomb and how Jesus' body was placed in it. ⁵⁶ Then they went back home and prepared the spices and perfumes for the body. On the Sabbath they rested, as the Law commanded.

Fill in the blanks as a family before you continue:

- At noon, the sky turned _____ and stayed that way until three o'clock.

    Answer: (dark)

- After Jesus died, a good man named _____ placed His body in a tomb.

    Answer: (Joseph)

- The women who followed Jesus saw where He was placed and prepared _____ and perfumes for His body.

    Answer: (spices)

Family and Kid-Friendly Questions for Discussion

1. Why did Jesus stay quiet when people lied about Him?

    Parent/Adult Tip: Jesus's silence shows strength, not weakness. This is a great time to talk to kids about how not everything needs a response. God's truths are what matter, not whatever one else says. Jesus trusted God more than defending Himself. Use this to teach self-control and faith in God's justice.

    Ask: What do you feel when someone says something untrue about you? Can staying quiet sometimes be stronger than shouting back? How can we ask God to help us respond in peace? Why do we feel the need to constantly defend ourselves when God is our defender?

2. What do you think Pilate felt when he couldn't find anything wrong with Jesus?

Parent/Adult Tip: Talk about how sometimes people know the right thing but are afraid to act on it. Peer pressure is real and can affect how we handle different situations. Encourage teens to be bold in truth, even when it's hard. Parent/Adults, this is a good time to share about times in your life when you wanted to speak up but didn't.

Ask: What stops people from doing the right thing? Can you think of a time you wanted to speak up but didn't? How does God help us when we feel unsure?

3. Jesus forgave the people who crucified Him. How is that possible?

    Parent/Adult Tip: Forgiveness is hard for both adults and kids. Use Jesus's act of forgiveness to show that forgiveness is a choice rooted in love, not fairness.

    Ask: Why do you think Jesus forgave them? Who is hard for you to forgive right now? How does God help us forgive when it's really tough? How does the story of Jesus's crucifixion help us forgive others?

4. One criminal asked Jesus to remember him. How did Jesus respond?

    Parent/Adult Tip: Reinforce the truth that Jesus's love isn't based on our past but on our hearts turning to Him. It's never too late to follow Jesus. The man on the cross next to Jesus had lived a life of sin, but he turned to Jesus before he died and joined Him in paradise.

Ask: What does this teach us about God's forgiveness? Do you think someone could come to Jesus even in their final days? How do we show we want to follow Him today?

> **Closing Prayer:** *Lord, thank You for the cross. Thank You for forgiving us like You forgave those around You, even as You suffered. Help our hearts stay soft and thankful for Your amazing grace. In Your name, we pray. Amen.*

Day 24

Luke 24 – Jesus Is Alive!

Challenge: Can anyone say the memory verse without looking it up? Repeat the memory verse as a family.

Memory Verse of the Week: *"In the same way, God's angels are happy when even one sinner turns to him"* (Luke 15:10).

> **Opening Prayer:** *Jesus, You are a living God! Your Word shows us the joy and hope that come with Your resurrection. Help our family feel that joy today and share it with others. As we have learned about Your life and great miracles, I pray our family continues to choose You in everything we do. In Your name, we pray. Amen.*

Luke 24:1-12

¹Very early on Sunday morning the women went to the tomb, carrying the spices they had prepared. ² When they found the stone rolled away from the entrance, ³ they went in. But they did not find the body of the Lord Jesus, ⁴ and they did not know what to think. Suddenly two men in shining white clothes stood beside them. ⁵ The women were afraid and bowed to the ground. But the men said, "Why are you looking in the place of the dead for someone who is alive? ⁶ Jesus isn't here! He has been raised from death. Remember that while he was still in Galilee, he told you, ⁷ 'The Son of Man will be handed over to sinners who will nail him to a cross. But three days later he will rise to life.'" ⁸ Then they remembered what Jesus had said. ⁹⁻¹⁰ Mary Magdalene, Joanna, Mary the mother of James, and some other women were the ones who had gone to the tomb. When they returned, they told the eleven apostles and the others what had happened. ¹¹ The apostles thought it was all nonsense, and they would not believe. ¹² But Peter ran to the tomb. And when he stooped down and looked in, he saw only the burial clothes. Then he returned, wondering what had happened.

Fill in the blanks as a family before you continue:

- The women did not find Jesus's _____ and did not know what to think.

Answer: (body)

- Jesus told his disciples, "The Son of Man will be handed over to _____ who will nail him to a cross. But three days later he will rise to _____."

  Answer: (sinners, life)

Luke 24:13-24

[13] That same day two of Jesus' disciples were going to the village of Emmaus, which was about eleven kilometers from Jerusalem. [14] As they were talking and thinking about what had happened, [15] Jesus came near and started walking along beside them. [16] But they did not know who he was. [17] Jesus asked them, "What were you talking about as you walked along?" The two of them stood there looking sad and gloomy. [18] Then the one named Cleopas asked Jesus, "Are you the only person from Jerusalem who didn't know what was happening there these last few days?" [19] "What do you mean?" Jesus asked. They answered: Those things that happened to Jesus from Nazareth. By what he did and said he showed that he was a powerful prophet, who pleased God and all the people. [20] Then the chief priests and our leaders had him arrested and sentenced to die on a cross. [21] We had hoped that he would be the one to set Israel free! But it has already been three days since all this happened. [22] Some women in our group surprised us. They had gone to the tomb early in the morning, [23] but did not find the body of Jesus. They came back, saying they had seen a vision of angels who told them that he is alive. [24] Some men from our group went to the tomb and found it just as the women had said. But they didn't see Jesus either.

Luke 24 – Jesus Is Alive!

Fill in the blanks as a family before you continue:

- Two of Jesus's followers were walking to a village called _____.

    Answer: (Emmaus)

- As they walked, they were talking about everything that had _____.

    Answer: (happened)

- They were sad because they had hoped Jesus would be the one to set _____ free.

    Answer: (Israel)

Luke 24:25-35

²⁵ Then Jesus asked the two disciples, "Why can't you understand? How can you be so slow to believe all that the prophets said? ²⁶ Didn't you know that the Messiah would have to suffer before he was given his glory?" ²⁷ Jesus then explained everything written about himself in the Scriptures, beginning with the Law of Moses and the Books of the Prophets. ²⁸ When the two of them came near the village where they were going, Jesus seemed to be going farther. ²⁹ They begged him, "Stay with us! It's already late, and the sun is going down." So Jesus went into the house to stay with them. ³⁰ After Jesus sat down to eat, he took some bread. He blessed it and broke it. Then he gave it to them. ³¹ At once they knew who he was, but he disappeared. ³² They said to each other, "When he talked with us along the road and explained the

Scriptures to us, didn't it warm our hearts?" ³³ So they got up and returned to Jerusalem. The two disciples found the eleven apostles and the others gathered together. ³⁴ And they learned from the group that the Lord was really alive and had appeared to Peter. ³⁵ Then the disciples from Emmaus told what happened on the road and how they knew he was the Lord when he broke the bread.

Fill in the blanks as a family before you continue:

- Jesus said to his disciples, "Didn't you know that the _____ would have to suffer before he was given his glory?"

    Answer: (messiah)

- On the Road to Emmaus, Jesus "explained everything written about himself in the Scriptures, beginning with the Law of _____ and the Books of the Prophets."

    Answer: Moses

    The disciples recognized Jesus when He broke the _____ .

    Answer: (bread)

Luke 24:36-53

³⁶ While Jesus' disciples were talking about what had happened, Jesus appeared and greeted them. ³⁷ They were frightened and terrified because they thought they were seeing a ghost. ³⁸ But Jesus said, "Why are you so frightened? Why do you doubt? ³⁹ Look at my hands and my feet and see who I am! Touch me and find out for yourselves. Ghosts don't have flesh and bones as you see I have." ⁴⁰ After Jesus said

this, he showed them his hands and his feet. [41] The disciples were so glad and amazed that they could not believe it. Jesus then asked them, "Do you have something to eat?" [42] They gave him a piece of broiled fish. [43] He took it and ate it as they watched. [44] Jesus said to them, "While I was still with you, I told you that everything written about me in the Law of Moses, the Books of the Prophets, and in the Psalms had to happen." [45] Then he helped them understand the Scriptures. [46] He told them: The Scriptures say that the Messiah must suffer, then three days later he will rise from death. [47] They also say that all people of every nation must be told in my name to turn to God, in order to be forgiven. So beginning in Jerusalem, [48] you must tell everything that has happened. [49] I will send you the one my Father has promised, but you must stay in the city until you are given power from heaven. [50] Jesus led his disciples out to Bethany, where he raised his hands and blessed them. [51] As he was doing this, he left and was taken up to heaven. [52] After his disciples had worshiped him, they returned to Jerusalem and were very happy. [53] They spent their time in the temple, praising God.

Fill in the blanks as a family before you continue:

- To prove He was alive, Jesus showed them His _____ and His feet.

Answer: (hands)

- Jesus told His disciples that the Scriptures said the Messiah would suffer, die, and rise from the dead on the _____ day.

Answer: (third)

- As Jesus was being taken up to Heaven, He raised His hands and _____ them.

   Answer: (blessed)

Family and Kid-Friendly Questions for Discussion

1. Why were the women surprised when they found the tomb empty?

   Parent/Adult Tip: Use this moment to talk about what surprises us about God. Younger kids often respond to emotions and visuals, so describe the setting. With teens, connect it to moments when faith defies logic—times when miracles happen or when things work out one way when they should have gone a different way. If we think for a minute, we can recall many examples in our lives when God worked for us in a nonlogical way. This is a good time, Parent/Adults, to share what God has done for you that surprised you in the best way, also have kids think about a time God showed up and surprised them.

   Ask: What would you have done if you had been one of the women at the empty tomb? Why is it important that the tomb was empty? Has God ever surprised you in a good way?

2. What does the angel mean when he says, "He is not here! He has risen"?

   Parent/Adult Tip: Explain that this is the cornerstone of the Christian faith. For younger kids, talk about how Jesus keeps His promises. For older ones, invite reflection on the hope this gives us. Because Jesus gave his life for us and rose again, we can have eternal life with him. How amazing is that! The God we serve is **alive**; he's not in some grave like all the other "gods" as my pastor would say. His bones have never been found because the tomb is empty, and "He has risen."

Ask: What does it mean to you that Jesus is alive today? How does this make Christianity different from other beliefs? Why is this good news?

3. Why didn't the two disciples recognize Jesus on the road to Emmaus?

    Parent/Adult Tip: Sometimes, emotions like sadness or confusion can keep us from seeing clearly or seeing God in our situation. Discuss how that's true for all of us, especially when life is tough.

    Ask: Have you ever missed something important because you were upset or distracted? Maybe you took a test and even though you knew the subject matter, you could not focus long enough to answer the questions correctly because of distractions. How can we learn to notice Jesus even on hard days? What helps you remember that Jesus is close?

4. Why did Jesus show them His hands and feet?

    Parent/Adult Tip: Explain that this proves Jesus really died and came back to life. It's not a story; it's a real event. Also Jesus knows we are prone to doubt, and He wants to prove His love to us. If you were in the room with His disciples, wouldn't you want to see some proof? I mean this is a big deal...coming back to life! Kids need to know that our faith is rooted in truth, not make-believe. Jesus died and came back to life. That's the truth.

Ask: Why do you think Jesus wanted them to see His scars? How would that help them believe? Do you believe Jesus really came back to life? Why or why not?

5. What does it mean that Jesus "opened their minds" to understand Scripture?

    Parent/Adult Tip: The Bible can feel confusing, especially for kids and teens—and even for adults. Reassure your kids that it's okay to have questions and that God helps us understand over time. The way we understand the Bible more is by reading it more. Make sure to find a Bible version that you can understand. My favorite version for reading with my kids is the Contemporary English Version (CEV); I also like to read it in the New International Version (NIV). The important thing is to find a version you understand and keep reading; if you need to read the same chapter a couple of times, that is also helpful.

    Ask: Is there a Bible story that's hard to understand? What's one thing about God you'd like to learn more about? How can we ask God to help us understand His Word?

6. Jesus said that the Good News should be shared with all nations. How can our family help do that?

    Parent/Adult Tip: Your kids don't have to be missionaries to share the gospel. Every act of kindness, encouragement, or conversation can reflect Jesus. Let them brainstorm ways to be "on the great mission" God has called us to be on. My pastor once said, "Sometimes, the only Bible people read is you." God made us in his image, and we are a reflection of Him; let's be more like Jesus. I know it's hard, but thank God we have His strength to help us through.

Ask: Who do you know that might need to hear about Jesus? How can we share God's love at school, work, or in our neighborhood? What is one small thing we could do this week to be a light?

Closing Prayer: *Heavenly Father, thank You for the hope of Easter morning—that death was not the end but the beginning for us. Help us to live like people who believe in the resurrection. Fill our home with Your joy and peace. Holy Spirit, help us to spread the good news and be examples of Your light and love, Lord. Jesus, we thank You for the amazing life You lived and the examples You left for us to follow. We love You and thank You, Lord. In Your name, we pray. Amen.*

Chapter Activities and Recipes

This chapter includes activities and games designed to complement the readings and discussion outlined for each day of *Advent Bible Study*. Feel free to choose the activities and games your family prefers and do them along with the day's study, or use them separately as a time of review and reflection.

Day 1: Luke 1 - An Angel Brings Good News

Angel Wing Sugar Cookies

Recipe: Using sugar cookie dough (either store-bought or homemade), roll out the dough and cut into wing shapes. Bake and decorate with white icing and edible glitter or sprinkles.

Zechariah's Quiet Game

This is a quiet game with a twist. In Luke chapter 1, Zechariah had to wait until his son was born to speak again. If you are baking the sugar cookies, challenge the family to see who can be quiet the whole time they are baking. Or you could use another activity and then talk about how hard this probably was for Zechariah.

You could also just play an old school game of the quiet game and reward the winner with a prize.

Silent Charades

Play a game of charades, without speaking, emphasizing Zechariah's temporary muteness. Without speaking, act out a word or phrase that others can guess. Whoever guesses correctly then begins his or her turn. Write the following on paper for game:

- Sleeping
- Yawning
- Brushing teeth
- Running
- Drinking
- Eating
- Listening
- Smelling
- Shaving
- Washing
- Driving
- Thinking
- Calling someone on the phone
- Watching TV
- Swimming
- Stretching
- Jumping
- Cutting hair
- Looking through binoculars
- Reading a book

Animal Ideas

- Lion
- Dog
- Cat
- Pig
- Elephant
- Tiger
- Mouse
- Cow
- Sheep
- Horse
- Giraffe
- Monkey
- Chicken
- Duck
- Seal
- Bee
- Parrot
- Gorilla
- Snake
- Shark

Day 2: Luke 2 – The Birth of Jesus

Star Pancakes

Recipe: Make pancakes shaped like stars using cookie cutters, topped with powdered sugar and berries to remind each other of the Star of Bethlehem.

Shepherd's Hide and Seek

Hide a "baby Jesus" figure or a Bible and have family members search for Him, like the shepherds did.

Star Gazing Night

If possible, go outside and look at the stars, discussing the star that led the shepherds.

Day 3: Luke 3 – John Prepares the Way

John Dip (without bugs!)

Recipe: Mix honey and yogurt (we use dairy-free vanilla) to make a dip. Make the dip as sweet as you want and grab some graham crackers or apple slices to dip into the mix. Use as a reminder that John ate wild honey and locust as part of his diet.

Day 4: Luke 4 – Jesus Says No to Temptation

Power Smoothies

Create a healthy snack showing that Jesus had spiritual strength. You can use H-E-B Blendables Powerhouse Smoothies, which you can find in the frozen fruit grocery aisle ready to go. It contains red grapes, strawberries, blueberries, chopped kale (or chopped spinach), bananas, and raspberries. Just add water and blend.

Sword Fruit Skewers

Kids can stab grapes, strawberries, blackberries, and kiwi onto skewers while you talk about Jesus using God's Word as His defense like a sword.

Desert Walk

Take a silent walk, reflecting on Jesus's time in the wilderness.

Scripture Defense Drill

Practice finding Scriptures in the Bible to familiarize your family with where the different books are. Talk about the importance of knowing the Bible and remind the kids that Jesus used Scripture to resist temptation from the devil. So we should know the Bible just as Jesus did. Using the following Scriptures, have a contest to see who can find the selected Scripture first. Have the winner read the verse when they find it:

- Matthew 28:19
- 2 Corinthians 5:21
- John 3:16
- Proverbs 3:5
- Philippians 4:13
- Jeremiah 29:11
- Romans 8:28
- Philippians 4:8
- Romans 3:24
- Joshua 1:9

Day 5: Luke 5 – Jesus Chooses His Helpers

Goldfish Nets

As you read Luke chapter 5, you could have gold fish (any flavor you prefer) in a small plastic bag; the gold fish represent fish, and the baggy represent nets from when Jesus sent Simon (Peter) back to let down his nets.

Jesus Says

We have all played "Simon Says," but today we are going to play "Jesus says." Play the game, emphasizing the importance of following Jesus.

Roof-Dropping Drama

Act out the story of the friends lowering the paralyzed man through the roof. This is a great activity if used during youth Bible service.

Trust Walk

Blindfold one person and let a partner guide them using voice commands only. Relate this to how we follow Christ. We cannot see Him physically, so we need to listen to Him and obey His directions to get to a certain destination. Turn this into a competition and add some obstacles to get in the way.

Day 6: Luke 6 – Jesus Teaches About Love

Kindness Kabobs

Make fruit skewers to share. As you can tell, I love a good fruit kabob, lol. Pick your favorite fruits and talk about how we "stack" kindness in life. You could each make your own or pick someone to make them for your family.

Kindness Chain

Grab a sheet of paper and cut it into strips. Write down each act of kindness you do and create a kindness chain. In the evening review the acts of kindness each of you did that day. Add a link to the paper chain each time someone shows love. Do this throughout the whole study and watch the chain grow.

Day 7: Luke 7 – Jesus Helps and Heals

Medal Cookies

Cut your favorite cookie dough into circles and bake. Decorate the cookies like medals to represent the centurion's faith in Jesus.

Resurrection Raisin Bread

Pick your favorite brand (I love Sun-Maid Cinnamon Swirl Raisin Sliced Bread). Pop slices in the toaster and serve warm with honey butter to symbolize new life.

Sin and Forgiveness Water

Write sins on paper if you're comfortable doing so and drop the "sins" in a bowl of water and watch them dissolve.

Gratitude Drawing

Draw something you're thankful that Jesus forgave you for.

Hidden Light Hunt

Hide different objects (could be anything you choose). I like hiding the little Jesus figurines to make this activity harder. Turn off all the lights and use flashlights to represent letting your light shine and how we need God's light in this dark world. Make this into a competition to see who can find the most hidden objects.

Day 8: Luke 8 – Jesus's Power Over Nature

Faith Boat Sandwiches

Use hoagie rolls, pita halves, or hot dog buns (these make the best boats) and fill them you're your favorite sandwich fixings. Talk about the storm and disciples on the boat and how Jesus calms the storm.

Good Soil Garden Veggie Cups

Set up individual cups with ranch dressing, carrot sticks, celery, and peppers "growing" in them to represent "good soil." Talk about how we want to be "good soil" for God's Word.

Good Seed Plant

As a family, go to your local plant nursery and have each person pick a small plant. Then tend and care for the plant and watch it grow. Talk about how we need God's Word to help us grow and be good soil.

Day 9: Luke 9 - Jesus Feeds Thousands

Fish and Loaves Charcuterie Board

I love to have dinner on a charcuterie board with all kinds of snacks. If you don't have a board, you can use a baking pan or cutting board. Put goldfish crackers, fish sticks, and different dinner rolls with butter and jam. Talk about Jesus multiplying the fish and bread and how He shared a meal with 5000 followers.

Team Testimony Time

Pair up to share something God has done for you.

Day 10: Luke 10 - The Good Neighbor

Teamwork Tacos

Who doesn't love a good taco night?! Make tacos, or if you don't feel like cooking, hit up your favorite fast-food Mexican restaurant and buy some. Assemble tacos in pairs, showing how Jesus sent the 72 disciples out two-by-two.

Good Samaritan Granola Bars

Make extra bars to deliver to neighbors or someone in need. This recipe is from RachlMansfield website at https://rachlmansfield.com/5-ingredient-peanut-butter-granola-bars/:

- 1 cup of creamy peanut butter (or any nut butter you prefer)
- ⅔ cup of honey
- 1 teaspoon of vanilla extract
- ½ teaspoon of sea salt

- 2 ½ cups of rolled oats
- 3 tablespoons of chopped nuts or seeds (I love pumpkin)
- ⅓ cup of dark chocolate morsels

Also I like to add dried cranberries or raisins, but those are totally optional.

Mix ingredients together in a bowl. Then pour the mixture into a pan lined with parchment paper. Freeze for at least an hour; then cut into bars. These are great to put in baggies and pass out to friends or the homeless.

Day 11: Luke 11 - Teach Us to Pray

Prayer Pretzels

I don't have a recipe for pretzels, but Target has some frozen pretzel bites, Auntie Anne's Classic Soft Frozen Pretzels (any brand will do). The twist shape reminds us of folded hands when we pray. This would be a great time to practice the Lord's prayer. Enjoy pretzels with your favorite dip, cheese, marinara, or chocolate.

Prayer Journals

Buy spirals and decorate with stickers or markers; use the journal for family prayers.

Day 12: Luke 12 - Don't Worry

Don't Worry, Trust Jesus, Nacho Heart

Individual nacho bowls are great for reminding kids not to worry and trust in God.

Ingredients: tortilla chips, Velveeta cheese, milk, ground beef, and any other toppings you would like (guacamole, sour cream, onions, beans, jalapenos, and so on).

Melt the Velveeta cheese and half a cup of milk (add more if needed). Once it's melted to your liking, pour over tortilla chips; add your toppings and enjoy!

Bird Watch Walk

Go on a walk as a family and look for birds and talk about God's care.

Pack for Heaven

As a family, share what you would take to Heaven if you could take one thing. What's really important in life? Talk about how treasure here on earth cannot be taken to Heaven and that what's really important is how we treat others and follow God's Word.

Worry-Free Balloon Pop

Write worries on balloons and pop them together symbolizing the release and giving up your worries to God.

Day 13: Luke 13 - God's Growing Kingdom

Fig Newtons and Healing Honey Lemon Tea

Nature's Bakery Fig bar is my favorite brand, but you could choose what you like. Grab some fig bars to enjoy as a treat as you talk about the story of the fig tree, which is mentioned in Jesus's teachings. Discuss what it means to be fruitful.

Grab some chamomile tea and add honey and lemon. Steep the

tea for about eight minutes before drinking; then add the honey and lemon (to your liking). While sipping warm, sweet tea. talk about Jesus healing the bent woman.

Faith Like a Mustard Seed

Purchase mustard seeds from your local Walmart or order them from Amazon. Look at the size of the mustard seeds; plant the seeds and talk about faith grows as you watch your mustard plant grow.

Day 14: Luke 14 – A Special Invitation

Salt of the Earth Popcorn

Grab your favorite popcorn and lightly salt it. Talk about how we flavor the world. We are the salt of the earth.

Invitation Craft

Create invitation cards for Jesus's kingdom using construction paper. Get creative as possible. Buy glitter and stickers.

Day 15: Luke 15 – The Lost and Found

Lost Coin Chocolate Hunt

Buy some chocolate coins and hide them around the house (not too many, you could make this a competition to see who finds the most coins). Talk about rejoicing when something that was lost is found just as Jesus rejoices when the "lost" find him. Then enjoy your lost chocolate coins as a sweet treat.

Celebrate Dance Party

Put on some worship and praise music and rejoice like the father in the story of the prodigal son. Our favorite right now is "No One" by Elevation Worship.

Day 16: Luke 16 - Being Faithful

Lazarus's Lentil Soup

This is a warm and humble meal to be served with bread. This is a great time to talk about staying humble and helping others in need. This crockpot recipe is from the Real Food Whole Life website at https://realfoodwholelife.com/.

Ingredients

- 1 medium yellow onion, chopped
- 1 cup chopped celery
- 2 cups chopped carrot
- 2 cloves garlic, minced or finely grated
- 2 teaspoons kosher salt, divided
- 1 ½ cups dry green lentils (or brown lentils)
- 1 (15-oz) can petite, diced tomatoes
- 6–8 cups vegetable stock
- 1 large bay leaf, or 2 small bay leaves

Cover and cook on high for 4–6 hours or on low for 6–8 hours, or until the veggies and lentils are soft. Add spinach the last hour. If you want to blend to make soup creamy, you can.

At the end, add 4 cups baby spinach and 1 teaspoon red wine vinegar. Drizzle with olive oil and serve.

Giving Jar

Grab a jar or bucket and start a giving jar for your house. Kids can put a penny, a dime, a dollar, or whatever they have that day or week. After your timeline is up, go buy something that will help someone in need. This could be food for the homeless, flowers for someone at an elderly person's home, or this can be given as an offering at church; the possibilities are endless. Also if kids get an allowance for chores or have a job, this is a great time to talk about tithing the 10 percent that belongs to God.

Day 17: Luke 17 - The Grateful One

Thankful Turkey Wraps and Grateful Grape Cups

Make wraps with turkey and cheese (add any other toppings you like); talk about gratitude and what you are all thankful for. Use cups of your favorite grapes to discuss giving thanks like the healed man. You can do both activities together, or you can do them separately.

Thank You Notes

Write thank you notes to people in your life.

Gratitude Journal Time

Take five minutes or more and write about something you are thankful for in your prayer notebook. Take this time to list a couple daily blessings.

Day 18: Luke 18 - Come to Jesus

Humble Pie (Mini Hand Pies)

Fun reminder that Jesus honors humble hearts. Talk about what having a humble heart looks like. You can either buy the mini pies, or make your own as a family. Here's an air fryer recipe from Pillsbury's website:

- Pillsbury pie crusts (cut into fours like a pizza)
- 2/3 cup of whatever pie filling you prefer (from a 21-oz can)
- 1 tablespoon butter, melted
- 1/2 teaspoon sugar

Using a spoon, put a small amount of filling in the middle of each triangle crust. Fold the crust in half over the filling; press edges firmly with fork to seal. Prick tops with fork to vent. Brush with melted butter, and sprinkle with sugar. Set air fryer to 350°F; place two hand pies in the air fryer basket, and cook for 11 to 18 minutes or until golden brown.

Day 19: Luke 19 - Jesus Loves Everyone

Tree-Top Fruit Stacks

Grab your favorite fruit snacks. My favorite brand is YumEarth or Annies. Stack fruit snack pieces as high as you can, like Zacchaeus climbing a tree. Make it a competition before you enjoy it. Talk about how persistent Zacchaeus was to see Jesus; he didn't let anything stand in his way.

Donkey Relay

Do piggyback rides representing Jesus riding into Jerusalem on a donkey.

Day 20: Luke 20 - Listening to Jesus

Cornerstone Crackers

Use square crackers to discuss Jesus as the cornerstone. Enjoy the crackers with some cheese and grapes for a nice snack.

Bold Berries Mix

Mix bright blackberries, strawberries, and raspberries in a bowl as a reminder to be bold in your faith like Jesus.

Day 21: Luke 21 - Jesus is Coming Again

Widow's Mite Mini Muffins

Bake tiny muffins (or buy the "little bites" muffin packs at the store) to represent the widow's small but powerful offering. Talk about how little can become much in God's hands.

Peace in the Storm Hot Cocoa

Warm up with hot cocoa and mini marshmallows. While drinking hot cocoa, talk about how Jesus promised peace even when the world feels shaky.

Widow's Offering Gift

Have children and parents come up with an offering or a gift to God. This does not have to be money but could be something important to them like a stuffed animal or a picture they drew or colored. Donate any toys or money that the family offered on the night of this activity.

Day 22: Luke 22 – The Last Supper

Last Supper Bread and Grape Juice

Get your favorite bread, break it apart as Jesus did. Then have a cup of your favorite grape juice as you reflect on the last supper and what it must have been like for Jesus to know that this was his last meal in the flesh with his disciples.

Day 23: Luke 23 – Jesus Dies for Us

Cross Craft

Build or draw simple crosses.

Day 24: Luke 24 – Jesus Is Alive

Empty Tomb Rolls

Bake crescent rolls with marshmallows inside; the marshmallows disappear like body in the empty tomb.

Bible Trivia: Family Feud Style Rules

Great for two Teams – All Ages

Roles:

- **1 Host** – asks questions, tracks points, and keeps the game fair and fun.
- **2 Teams** – mix of ages encouraged!

Game Setup:

- Teams come up with fun **team names**.
- Host flips a coin or asks a "starter question" to decide who goes first.

How to Play:

1. **Ask the Question:**
   - Host reads a Bible trivia question. (Questions are listed after the rules.)
   - Team 1 gets first chance to answer.

2. **Answering:**
   - If Team 1 answers correctly → they earn 1 point.
   - If Team 1 answers wrong → Team 2 gets a chance to steal.

- If Team 2 answers correctly → they get the point.
- If both are wrong → no point awarded, host reveals answer.

3. **Rotate Turns:**
   - After each question, alternate which team gets first attempt.
   - If Team 1 gets a question wrong and Team 2 answers correctly, it is still Team 2's turn.

   If both Teams get the answers wrong, continue to go in order. Even though Team 2 answered last, Team 1 got their original question wrong, so it will still be Team 2's question next.

4. **Bonus Round Option (Optional):**
   - Every fifth question can be a **bonus question** worth **2 points**.

Winning:

- Team with the most points at the end of the 20 questions wins! If you want to make some questions (maybe every fifth question) worth double or more points you can; this will be up to the "host."
- Option: Let the winning team pick the next family movie night, dessert, or get Bible Bucks!

Rules:

- No shouting out answers. Must be a new person giving the answer to each question; I would go with shortest to tallest or by age.
- Teams can discuss for up to **20 seconds** before answering.

- No Bibles or phones allowed during play.
- Be encouraging! Praise good effort and teamwork.

Parent/Adult Tip: Turn incorrect answers into learning moments. After revealing the answer, briefly explain the story or meaning, and invite a quick reflection.

Luke 1-6 Trivia

Answers bolded with full explanation next to them:

1. Who appeared to Zechariah in the temple? **Gabriel** (The angel Gabriel told him about John's birth.)

2. What was the name of John's mother? **Elizabeth** (She was a relative of Mary and wife to Zechariah.)

3. Who was Mary engaged to? **Joseph** (He was from the family line of David.)

4. What town was Jesus born in? **Bethlehem** (Joseph took Mary there for the census.)

5. What did Mary place baby Jesus in? **Manger** (There was no room in the inn.)

6. Who were the first people to hear about Jesus's birth from angels? **Shepherds** (They were watching their flocks at night.)

7. Who blessed baby Jesus in the temple and said he could now die in peace? **Simeon** (He had been waiting for the Messiah.)

8. What prophetess also saw baby Jesus in the temple? **Anna** (She praised God and told others about Jesus.)

9. How old was Jesus when His parents found Him in the temple? **Twelve** (He had stayed behind in Jerusalem.)

10. What was John's mission? **Prepare the way for Jesus** (He came to prepare the way for the Lord.)

11. What animal is John the Baptist associated with wearing? **Camel** (He wore clothes made of camel's hair.)

12. What did John baptize people in? **Water, in the Jordan River** (He baptized in the Jordan River.)

13. What descended like a dove when Jesus was baptized? **Holy Spirit** (The Holy Spirit came down from Heaven.)

14. How many days did Jesus fast in the wilderness? **Forty** (He was tempted by the devil for forty days.)

15. Where was Jesus rejected by the people? **Nazareth** (His hometown did not accept Him.)

16. What evil being did Jesus command to leave a man in the synagogue? **Demon** (It came out, and everyone was amazed.)

17. What was Peter doing when Jesus told him to let down his nets again? **Fishing** (He had fished all night and caught nothing.)

18. What disease did Jesus heal when He touched a man and said, "Be clean"? **Leprosy** (The man was immediately healed.)

19. How did friends bring a paralyzed man to Jesus when the house was crowded? **Roof** (They lowered him through the roof.)

20. Who did Jesus say He came to call to turn from their sins? **Sinners** ("Healthy people don't need a doctor.")

Luke 7-12 Trivia

Answers bolded with full explanation next to them:

1. Who healed the centurion's servant? **Jesus** (Jesus healed him with just a word.)

2. What city did Jesus raise the widow's son in? **Nain** (Jesus saw the funeral in the town of Nain.)

3. Who sent messengers to ask Jesus if He was the one they were waiting for? **John** (John the Baptist from prison.)

4. What did the sinful woman use to dry Jesus's feet? **Hair** (She wept, washed His feet, and dried them with her hair.)

5. What kind of ground is mentioned in the parable of the sower of seeds? Must name all four: **good ground, rocky ground, thorny, dry path** (In good ground, seeds grew and produced. In rocky ground, seeds started growing but dried up. In thorny ground, weeds grew up and choked the plants. On the path, seeds were trampled on and eaten by birds.)

6. Who did Jesus raise back to life in Luke? **Girl (Jairus's daughter.)**

7. What did Jesus feed over 5,000 people with? **Bread and fish** (Bread and fish were multiplied with baskets of food left over.)

8. Who said, "You are the Messiah sent from God"? **Peter** (He confessed Jesus as the Christ.)

9. What did Jesus's clothes look like when He was transfigured? **Shining brightly** (His clothes became as bright as lightning.)

10. What spirit did Jesus cast out from a boy? **Demon** (The boy was possessed and often thrown into convulsions.)

11. How many people did Jesus send out in pairs? **Seventy-two**

12. What parable teaches us to love our neighbor? **Samaritan** (The Good Samaritan helped the injured man.)

13. Which sister sat at Jesus's feet to listen? **Mary** (While Martha was busy, Mary listened.)

14. What prayer did Jesus teach His disciples? **Lord's Prayer** (The Lord's Prayer begins "Father, help us to honor your name.")

15. Recite the Lord's Prayer. Here are two versions from Scripture:

Our Father in heaven, hallowed be your name, your kingdom come, your will be done, on earth as it is in heaven. Give us today our daily bread. And forgive us our debts, as we also have forgiven our debtors. And lead us not into temptation, but deliver us from the evil one.

—Matthew 6:9–13 NIV

Our Father, which art in heaven, Hallowed be thy Name. Thy kingdom come. Thy will be done in earth as it is in heaven. Give us this day our daily bread. And forgive us our debts , as we forgive our debtors. And lead us not into temptation, but deliver us from evil: For Thine is the kingdom, and the power, and the glory, for ever Amen.

—Matthew 6:9–13 KJV

16. Who did Jesus warn the people not to be like in their hypocrisy? **Pharisees** (They looked good outwardly but were inwardly corrupt.)

17. How many sparrows are sold for two coins? **Five** (Jesus reminded them of their value to God.)

18. What sin does Jesus say cannot be forgiven? **Blasphemy** (Specifically blasphemy against the Holy Spirit.)

19. What are we supposed to store up in Heaven? **Heavenly Treasure** (He taught about storing heavenly treasures.)

20. What does Jesus say we should always be ready for? **His Return** (He told them to be ready for the Master's return.)

Luke 13-18 Trivia

Answers bolded with full explanation next to them:

1. What kind of tree did Jesus mention as not producing fruit?

   Answer: Fig (Jesus used the fig tree to teach that we should produce good fruit (godly actions) in our lives, or we risk being cut off.)

2. What day did Jesus heal a crippled woman, causing outrage?

   Answer: Sabbath (Jesus healed her on the Sabbath, challenging the idea that doing good was "work" and showing that helping people matters to God.)

3. Jesus compared the Kingdom of God to what small seed?

   Answer: Mustard (The mustard seed shows that God's kingdom starts small but grows into something great.)

4. What kind of door did Jesus say people should try to enter through?

   Answer: Narrow (Not everyone can go through "the narrow door.")

5. Who did Jesus call a "fox"?

   Answer: Herod (Jesus used "fox" to describe Herod's cunning and untrustworthy nature, warning of corrupt leadership.)

6. On the sabbath at the home of an important Pharisee, Jesus healed a man with what condition?

   Answer: swollen legs (Jesus showed compassion despite Pharisees watching Him.)

7. Jesus said not to take the best what at a banquet?

   Answer: Seat (This was about humility.)

8. In the parable of the great feast, people made what?

   Answer: Excuses (They refused the invitation, symbolizing people who ignore God's call because of worldly distractions.)

9. Jesus said we must carry what to be His disciple?

   Answer: Cross (A symbol of surrender and sacrifice)

10. What did the shepherd leave behind to find one lost sheep?

    Answer: Ninety-nine sheep (He seeks even one lost soul because they matter deeply to Him.)

11. What did the woman search for in Luke 15?

    Answer: Coin (Represents how God searches for the lost and celebrates when someone turns back to Him.)

12. In the story of the prodigal son, what did the younger son ask for?

    Answer: Inheritance (Asking early was disrespectful, but this story shows how God welcomes us back even when we've walked away.)

13. What did the prodigal son feed when he had no food?

    Answer: Pigs (Feeding pigs was especially shameful, showing how low the son had fallen before going back.)

14. The older brother became what when the father celebrated?

    Answer: Angry (He didn't understand grace. Jesus showed that we shouldn't be jealous when others receive forgiveness.)

15. In Luke 16, what was the dishonest manager managing?

    Answer: Money (Jesus used this to teach about stewardship and being faithful with what God gives us.)

16. Who begged for water in the parable of the rich man and Lazarus?

    Answer: Rich man (After death, the rich man suffered and wanted relief, but Jesus showed it was too late for him to change his heart.)

17. Jesus said if someone sins and repents, we must do what?

    Answer: Forgive (No matter how many times someone messes up, Jesus wants us to forgive, just as God forgives us.)

18. How many times did Jesus say we should forgive in one day?

    Answer: Seven (This shows ongoing forgiveness.)

19. How many lepers did Jesus heal in Luke 17?

    Answer: Ten (All were healed.)

20. How many of those healed lepers came back to thank Jesus?

    Answer: One (The one who returned was a Samaritan.)

Luke 19-24 Trivia

Answers bolded with full explanation next to them:

1. Who climbed a tree to see Jesus?

   Answer: Zacchaeus (He was a short tax collector who wanted to see Jesus.)

2. What kind of tree did Zacchaeus climb?

   Answer: Sycamore (This tree was common in the region, perfect for climbing and seeing over a crowd.)

3. Jesus said the temple had become a den of what?

   Answer: Thieves (People were using God's house for dishonesty, and Jesus cleared it out to restore it as a place of worship.)

4. What animal did Jesus ride into Jerusalem?

   Answer: Donkey/Colt (Fulfilling prophecy, Jesus entered humbly on a donkey.)

5. The crowd shouted what word when Jesus entered Jerusalem?

   Answer: Hosanna (The people welcomed Jesus as King.)

6. What did Jesus do to the tables in the temple?

   Answer: Overturned/flipped them (He flipped the tables of the money-changers to show His anger.)

7. What did Jesus say would cry out if His followers were silent?

   Answer: Stones/rocks (Creation itself would praise Jesus if people didn't.)

Bible Trivia

8. Who betrayed Jesus for money?

    Answer: Judas (He was one of Jesus's disciples but chose to betray Him.)

9. How many pieces of silver did Judas receive?

    Answer: Thirty (This fulfilled prophecy.)

10. At the Last Supper, what did Jesus break and give to His disciples?

    Answer: Bread (It symbolized His body, broken for us.)

11. After the supper, Jesus also shared what with His disciples?

    Answer: Cup (The cup symbolized His blood, shed for the forgiveness of sins.)

12. Where did Jesus go to pray before He was arrested?

    Answer: Garden of Gethsemane (A garden where Jesus asked God for strength.)

13. Who cut off a servant's ear during Jesus's arrest?

    Answer: Peter (Peter was a gangster. He tried to defend Jesus, but Jesus healed the ear and chose not to fight back.)

14. Who denied Jesus three times?

    Answer: Peter (He denied him three times before the rooster crowed.)

15. What did the soldiers place on Jesus's head?

    Answer: Crown of Thorns (A crown of thorns mocked Jesus's claim to be King.)

16. Who was released instead of Jesus?

    Answer: Barabbas (A murderer who was set free when the crowd chose to have Jesus crucified instead.)

17. What did Jesus carry to the place of His crucifixion?

    Answer: Cross (He carried the cross part of the way before Simon helped.)

18. Where was Jesus crucified?

    Answer: Golgotha/The Skull (It was the place of execution outside Jerusalem.)

19. What happened in the temple when Jesus died?

    Answer: Curtain/veil tore (The thick temple curtain tore in two, showing that access to God was now open through Jesus.)

20. Who found the empty tomb first?

    Answer: Women (Women like Mary Magdalene were the first witnesses to Jesus's resurrection.)

Endnotes

1. Philip Anthony Mitchell, Sermon, "So We Fasted," 2819 Church, Atlanta, Georgia, January 6, 2025.

2. Mitchell, "So We Fasted."

3. "What Are Spiritual Gifts? Impact Nations, accessed July 17, 2025, https://www.impactnations.com/blogs/article-what-are-spiritual-gifts?gad_source=1&gad_campaignid=21184565457&gbraid=0AAAAADlC6EcHQMNbWLZMseTLnq_3Cwg6m&gclid=CjwKCAjwvuLDBhAOEiwAPtF0Vu8PMck8AYzzN-JRgoQIt_9LTt_05YiJ7ualhuaZ22ikAczy4RUQbWBoC5G-gQAvD_BwE.

4. Manny Arango, "Luke & Acts Arma Bible Study Courses," accessed July 2025, https://www.armacourses.com/.

www.ingramcontent.com/pod-product-compliance
Lightning Source LLC
Chambersburg PA
CBHW070530090426
42735CB00013B/2932